I0002383

QWEN2.5-MAX GUIDEBOOK

GUIDEBOOK

Your Essential Manual for Enhanced
Performance

BEN TAYLOR

Copyright © 2025 **Ben Taylor**

All Rights Reserved

The publisher grants no authorization for the complete book or partial content to reproduce by electronic means including photocopy, recording or otherwise except when permitted through US copyright law and fair use standards.

Disclaimer and Terms of Use

The author together with the publisher have applied their absolute dedication in creating this book while producing its supporting materials. The author together with the publisher decline all responsibility for correctness along with applicability and suitability and completeness of contents in this book. This document contains information only for informational purposes. The acceptance of full accountability for your decisions and actions comes with choosing to implement any concepts from this book.

This book received printing services in the United States of America.

TABLE OF CONTENTS

CHAPTER ONE 4

INTRODUCTION 5

Overview of Qwen 2.5-Max 5

Key Features & Capabilities of Qwen 2.5-Max........................8

CHAPTER TWO...16

GETTING STARTED 16

Installation & Setup for Qwen 2.5-Max 16

Accessing the Model (API, CLI, Web UI)........................25

CHAPTER THREE 35

MODEL SPECIFICATIONS 35

Architecture & Parameters of Qwen 2.5-Max 35

Supported Languages & Tasks in Qwen 2.5-Max....................46

CHAPTER FOUR...59

USAGE GUIDE 59

Basic Prompting Techniques for Qwen 2.5-Max....................59

Advanced Features of Qwen 2.5-Max: Multi-turn Dialogue &
Tool Usage 68

CHAPTER FIVE...79

API & INTEGRATION 79

API Endpoints & Authentication for Qwen 2.5-Max 79

Python SDK Examples for Qwen 2.5-Max 90

CHAPTER SIX...101

FINE-TUNING & CUSTOMIZATION 101

Adapting Qwen 2.5-Max for Specific Tasks...........................101

CHAPTER SEVEN 113

PERFORMANCE OPTIMIZATION 113

Speed vs. Accuracy Trade-offs in Qwen 2.5-Max.....................113

Hardware Recommendations for Qwen 2.5-Max...................123

CHAPTER EIGHT 135

TROUBLESHOOTING & FAQS..135

Common Issues & Solutions for Qwen 2.5-Max 135

CHAPTER NINE..148

ETHICS & SAFETY 148

Responsible AI Guidelines for Qwen 2.5-Max 148

CHAPTER TEN 159

RESOURCES & SUPPORT 159

Official Documentation Links for Qwen 2.5-Max.....................159

Qwen 2.5-Max Community Forums...162

CHAPTER ONE

INTRODUCTION

Overview of Qwen 2.5-Max

Qwen 2.5-Max stands as the enhanced edition of the Qwen AI language model that brings about stronger functionality and capability along with higher operational performance across all platforms. Qwen 2.5-Max uses state-of-the-art deep learning principles that enable real-time human-like responses to handle advanced queries.

Key Highlights of Qwen 2.5-Max:

1. **Advanced Natural Language Understanding**: Qwen 2.5-Max delivers improved natural language understanding capabilities which enables it to produce relevant coherent answers during complicated situations by understanding context and tone and intent more effectively.

2. **Faster and More Efficient**: The design of this model ensures fast query processing with small response times that makes it a great solution for real-time communication together with extensive high-speed deployments that require speed.

3. **Enhanced Fine-Tuning Capabilities**: Qwen 2.5-Max allows users to modify the model easier

according to their specific business requirements or target applications. Qwen 2.5-Max demonstrates superior versatility by fitting various operation settings including consumer assistance and content production and academic investigation.

4. **Expanded Multi-Language Support**: Qwen 2.5-Max delivers extended language understanding support which enables it to service worldwide customers through its multilingual capabilities.

5. **Context-Aware Responses**: Qwen 2.5-Max keeps track of session interactions since its prior use which enables dialogue continuity through context-aware response generation.

6. **Customization Options**: Users can transform Qwen 2.5-Max through business-led customization options for specified response adjustment or new domain knowledge integration or style modifications.

7. **Security and Privacy**: ecurity and Privacy stand as primary qualities of Qwen 2.5-Max because user contacts together with sensitive information remain thoroughly secured. Security protocols embedded in Qwen 2.5-Max provide protection against both

cyber thefts and intrusion attempts from unauthorized individuals.

8. **Scalability**: The software platform Qwen 2.5-Max supports workload flexibility by adjusting to projects ranging from small businesses to large corporate entities without affecting performance standards.

Target Audience for Qwen 2.5-Max:

- Business operations need AI-powered solutions to enhance their customer service operations and produce content as well as analyze data.

- The development team as well as researchers and developers need Qwen 2.5-Max to construct advanced AI models specifically for tasks including sentiment analysis text summarization and language translation.

- Educators together with Students represent the target audience that wants to use AI technology for interactive educational experiences along with problem-solving capabilities.

- Creative professionals utilize Qwen 2.5-Max for marketing, media and entertainment purposes to get inspiration or generate content with AI assistance.

Qwen 2.5-Max provides users with a powerful artificial intelligence solution that can transform productivity along with innovation across numerous sectors by uniting artificial intelligence capabilities with user-friendly features. The platform follows a user-friendly approach that services both beginner and expert users to let them reach their objectives quickly.

Key Features & Capabilities of Qwen 2.5-Max

Qwen 2.5-Max contains multiple innovative features that make it unique against other available language models. The platform demonstrates specific functional and operational elements which suit many sectors including automatic customer service applications and content creation situations and academic research needs. The main characteristics of Qwen 2.5-Max serve developers businesses while providing essential capabilities to individuals who need its powerful functionality.

1. Advanced Natural Language Processing (NLP)

- **Contextual Understanding**: Qwen 2.5-Max features better contextual understanding capabilities because it identifies hidden user intent within complex conversations. The system maintains a running context between different interactions which ensures it provides well-informed responses throughout a conversation.

- **Sentiment Analysis**: The system performs sentiment analysis to detect positive negative and neutral user sentiments and generates suitable responses thus delivering value to customer support service applications and social media monitoring along with content creation operations.

- **Multilingual Support**: The system provides multilingual support through Qwen 2.5-Max which enables smooth communication across various linguistic environments. The user interaction capabilities of Qwen 2.5-Max extend to major linguistic regions which cover primary languages including English, Spanish, French and Mandarin among others.

2. Customization and Fine-Tuning

- **Tailored Responses**: Qwen 2.5-Max allows users to customize its responses for specific industries by modifying response tone and style parameters as well as personality features to match targeted needs such as formal or casual communication (including technical and creative approaches).

- **Domain-Specific Knowledge**: The model accepts specialized datasets to build domain-specific understanding of specialized jargon and niche topics. Qwen 2.5-Max serves these industries flawlessly because of its ability to work with healthcare, finance, legal and education environments.

3. Real-Time Response Generation

- **Low Latency**: Qwen 2.5-Max features minimal delay processing to provide real-time communication for users through its low-latency response generation system. The requirement for real-time responses makes Qwen 2.5-Max ideal for applications requiring chatbots and virtual assistance services and interactive customer support.

- **High Throughput**: The model operates with high throughput capability which allows simultaneous query execution without performance decreases.

4. Robust Content Generation

- **Creative Content Generation**: Qwen 2.5-Max performs outstanding creative content generation to produce human-similar written articles and stories as well as marketing texts product descriptions among other creative written content. Through its design the model produces structured content that reads naturally and at length.

- **Summarization and Paraphrasing**: The model processes complex tasks by creating both summary reports from multi-page documents and accurate paraphrased content that preserves the original meaning in its output text.
- **Text Translation**: The system provides effective multilingual text translation which maintains original message content along with its intended tone.

5. Advanced Query Handling

- **Complex Query Understanding**: The platform Qwen 2.5-Max processes sophisticated information requests with multiple layers which turns it into a suitable system for research assistance and technical support and data analysis tasks.
- **Search Integration**: Search Integration enables the model to interact with search engines and internal databases so it retrieves current data for knowledge management system applications.

6. Scalability and Deployment

- **Cloud-Ready Architecture**: Qwen 2.5-Max incorporates a cloud-ready architecture that allows businesses to run it on cloud infrastructure for scalable deployments between small-scale apps and enterprise-level systems.

- **Multi-Platform Support**: Qwen 2.5-Max allows deployment on wcb applications and mobile apps together with IoT devices and embedded systems providing organizations with deployment flexibility across different environments.

7. Enhanced Security and Privacy

- **Data Encryption**: Qwen 2.5-Max allows deployment on web applications and mobile apps together with IoT devices and embedded systems providing organizations with deployment flexibility across different environments.

- **Privacy-Preserving Features**: The demonstrate gives privacy-protecting measures through industry-standard hones that stow away users' character by utilizing anonymization strategies whereas guaranteeing privacy in all intuitive. The framework gives back for GDPR control compliance in expansion to other protection measures.

- **Access Control**: Through its system the show gives total information get to administration which grants exact under staking of authorized staff and limited person get to private substance.

8. Seamless Integration

- **API and SDK Support**: Through its API and SDK support platform Qwen 2.5-Max allows easy combination of its capabilities into users' existing workflows and systems through its robust programming standards.

- **Plugin Support**: Through its API and SDK support platform Qwen 2.5-Max allows easy combination of its capabilities into users' existing workflows and systems through its robust programming standards.

- **Cross-Platform Integration**: The solution enables seamless integration through plugin support for widely used services including Microsoft Teams followed by Slack so Qwen 2.5-Max can be easily incorporated into existing platforms.

9. Robust Analytics and Reporting

- **Insights Generation**: Qwen 2.5-Max generates powerful analytics to show users how well their responses perform together with different engagement patterns and additional essential metrics.

- **Performance Monitoring**: The built-in tools let users check system performance together with usage statistics for system optimization through time.

10. Error Handling and Fault Tolerance

- **Resilience to Errors**: The system delivers fault tolerance capabilities along with error-resilience features to maintain operational sustainability when minor operational problems occur. The system needs this capability to keep running without interruption in vital mission applications.

- **Self-Healing Mechanisms**: Qwen 2.5-Max provides automatic features which detect minor problems to resolve them independently without administrator action which reduces manual troubleshooting needs.

Summary

Qwen 2.5-Max stands as an exceptionally progressed AI demonstrate that provides comprehensive highlights which clients can utilize for different purposes. Qwen 2.5-Max highlights broad capabilities which incorporate dealing with complex intelligent through characteristic dialect handling along side highlights like customization alternatives and real-time preparing and multilingual bolster. Users working on chatbot development or content generation or enterprise AI implementations must consider Qwen 2.5-Max because it fulfills all needs while providing secure and efficient performance.

CHAPTER TWO

GETTING STARTED

Installation & Setup for Qwen 2.5-Max

To establish Qwen 2.5-Max operations you need to follow specific procedures that start with preparation of your environment along with component installation. The installation procedure works smoothly regardless of your intention to deploy Qwen 2.5-Max on either local equipment or cloud infrastructure. The following steps outline the process of setting up Qwen 2.5-Max installation and configuration.

1. System Requirements

The installation process requires checking that your system fulfills these system prerequisites:

- **Operating System**:
  - Linux (Ubuntu recommended)
  - macOS (Mojave or later)
  - Windows 10 or later
- **Hardware Requirements**:
  - **CPU**: Minimum of 4 cores, preferably 8 or more cores for better performance.

- o **RAM**: For maximum efficiency it is recommended to install Qwen 2.5-Max with 16 GB of RAM while the minimum requirement is 8 GB.
- o **Disk Space**: At least 20 GB of free disk space for installation and dependencies.
- **Software Requirements**:
  - o Python 3.7 or later (Python 3.9 recommended)
  - o Docker (for containerized deployment)
  - o Node.js and npm (for web integration)
  - o Git (for version control)

2. Preparing Your Environment

Step 1: Install Python and Dependencies

To install Python choose these directions:

- For Ubuntu/Linux:
- sudo apt update
- sudo apt install python3 python3-pip python3-venv
- **For macOS**:
  - o Install Python via Homebrew:
  - o brew install python
- **For Windows**:
  - o Download the latest Python version from the official website.

- o Press on include Python to Way after you introduce the program.

Begin Python to affirm it works properly by entering this command within the terminal:

python3 --version

Step 2: Install Required Libraries

Qwen 2.5-Max requires a set of required bundles for its operation:

pip install --upgrade pip

pip install -r requirements.txt

Using Docker simplifies your work because the platform manages software requirements automatically instead of manual setup.

3. Installation via Docker (Recommended for Cloud/Containerized Environments)

Docker provides the best method to install and run Qwen 2.5-Max effectively. This setup strategy makes a ensured environment for Qwen 2.5-Max and conveys uniform framework comes about without disturbances.

Step 1: Install Docker

- For Ubuntu/Linux:
- sudo apt update
- sudo apt install docker.io
- sudo systemctl enable --now docker
- **For macOS**:
    o Get Docker by downloading it from its official website.
- **For Windows**:
    o Get the Docker Desktop setup by downloading it from this site.

Check whether Docker runs properly after installing it:

docker --version

Step 2: Pull the Docker Image for Qwen 2.5-Max

You can execute Docker after setting up by downloading the Qwen 2.5-Max version from its Docker repository service.

docker pull qwen/qwen-2.5-max:latest

Step 3: Run Qwen 2.5-Max in a Docker Container

You can start the container using the Docker image pull result once it is available:

docker run -d -p 5000:5000 qwen/qwen-2.5-max:latest

- The command starts Qwen 2.5-Max background operations (-d) and lets it connect to port 5000.

Step 4: Access Qwen 2.5-Max

After starting the container you can use HTTP and other system communication methods to work with Qwen 2.5-Max.

4. Installation via Python (For Local Development/Testing)

To install Qwen 2.5-Max locally follow the procedures below:

Step 1: Clone the Repository

Initiate the Qwen 2.5-Max source code project by either cloning its repository or downloading it from the specified URL:

git   clone   https://github.com/your-repository/qwen-2.5-max.git

cd qwen-2.5-max

Step 2: Set Up a Virtual Environment (Recommended)

Establishing a virtual environment keeps your project modules separate from other software:

python3 -m venv qwen-env

source qwen-env/bin/activate # For Linux/macOS

qwen-env\Scripts\activate # For Windows

Step 3: Install Dependencies

After turning on the virtual environment you should install all needed Python components:

pip install -r requirements.txt

Step 4: Configure the Application

Based on your project requirements you need to personalize the program setup by configuring settings in the application. Review the necessary setup steps in both the project documentation and its README file.

Step 5: Run Qwen 2.5-Max Locally

You can start Qwen 2.5-Max local execution by running its main Python script:

python3 app.py

This initializes the application and lets you access Qwen 2.5-Max through the terminal or web interface based on its design.

5. Configuration

Step 1: API Key and Authentication (If Applicable)

Begin by setting up the necessary API authorization related credentials if required. You need to set up API authentication methods in Qwen 2.5-Max when access permission requirements exist. Commonly this procedure requires modifying environment settings or making changes in configuration files.

For example:

trade QWEN_API_KEY="your_api_key_here"

Upgrade the settings specifically within the config registry.

Step 2: Fine-Tuning (Optional)

You ought to optimize the settings of Qwen 2.5-Max to match your application needs. You'll transfer preparing information whereas setting up framework choices and after that begin the preparing handle.

Step 3: Configure Networking (For Cloud or Production Use)

When you run Qwen 2.5-Max in the cloud or connect it with external applications select proper networking settings based on your cloud deployment approach.

6. Verify Installation

You can check if Qwen 2.5-Max meets your requirements through these steps:

- **For Docker**: container logs to see if Qwen 2.5-Max operates correctly.
- docker logs <container_id>
- **For Python**: When using Python on a local machine open any browser and test the API URL http://localhost:5000 or use curl to verify the response.

7. Updating Qwen 2.5-Max

Your Docker updates take place with a new Docker image pull or source code and dependency changes:

- For Docker:
- docker pull qwen/qwen-2.5-max:latest
- docker restart <container_id>
- For Local Python Setup:
- git pull origin main
- pip install --upgrade -r requirements.txt

8. Troubleshooting

- **Installation Errors**: Look at installation logs to find out if requirements are missing or conflicting.
- **Docker Issues**: Docker setup must support networking and port forwarding when connecting to external APIs.
- **API Key Issues**: Rephrase the configuration settings for key access issues when authentication fails.

Conclusion

You can set up Qwen 2.5-Max successfully either on your local PC or within cloud-based environments through these steps. You can run your projects successfully across both containerized Docker deployment and local Python development through Qwen 2.5-Max platform. You can find solutions in the troubleshooting part of our guide or read the official documentation when you need help installing Qwen 2.5-Max.

Accessing the Model (API, CLI, Web UI)

With Qwen 2.5-Max you have many choices to connect to the model based on your needs and preferences. Users can connect to Qwen 2.5-Max through API access as well as

CLI and Web UI. Your tasks with Qwen 2.5-Max depend on which access method you use because all interfaces let you utilize its capabilities effectively.

1. Accessing the Model via API

Using the API tool allows you to retrieve full functionality of Qwen 2.5-Max by sending HTTP commands to access its data.

Step 1: API Endpoints

Once you install Qwen 2.5-Max (either Dockered or through local Python) it will create API access points. The base URL for API usage will have this form:

- **Localhost**: http://localhost:5000
- **Production/Cloud**: The production/cloud URL for your system is available for use.

Following are the most popular API endpoints that serve as starting points for users to access Qwen 2.5-Max:

- **POST /query**: You can use POST /query to submit text and receive results from the model.
- **GET /status**: You can access API endpoint status by using GET /status.

Step 2: Making an API Request

You'll be able yield API calls to work with the show. Here is an illustration show of cURL and Python API demands.

Example Using cURL:

```
curl -X POST http://localhost:5000/query \
-H "Content-Type: application/json" \
-d '{"query": "What is the weather today?"}'
```

Example Using Python (requests library):

```
import requests
import json


url = "http://localhost:5000/query"
headers = {"Content-Type": "application/json"}
data = {"query": "What is the weather today?"}


response = requests.post(url, headers=headers, json=data)


print(response.json())
```

Step 3: Authentication (If Required)

You would like to send the API key interior the HTTP headers for Qwen 2.5-Max occurrences that confirm through API keys.

```
curl -X POST http://localhost:5000/query \
-H "Content-Type: application/json" \
-H "Authorization: Bearer your_api_key_here" \
-d '{"query": "What is the weather today?"}'
```

In the Python case you wish to include Authorization esteem as your_api_key_here:

```
headers = {
    "Content-Type": "application/json",
    "Authorization": "Bearer your_api_key_here"
}
```

Step 4: Response Format

The demonstrate for the most part conveys the produced yield through a JSON record structure. Illustration of a ordinary reaction:

Example of a typical response:

```
{
  The current climate appears sunny skies at 75°F nowadays
}
```

2. Accessing the Model via CLI (Command Line Interface)

Clients who need to utilize Qwen 2.5-Max through the terminal interface or script computerization discover the CLI interface valuable.

Step 1: Installing CLI Tools

Clients who run the model either locally or interior Docker get CLI apparatuses included with their establishment prepare. So also clients can introduce these apparatuses either amid Python bundle setup or afterward on.

For example:

```
pip install qwen-cli
```

Step 2: Using CLI to Query the Model

You'll be able run queries against Qwen 2.5-Max after having introduced its command line interface. You'll be able enter this arrange to send demands to Qwen 2.5-Max through CLI:

```
qwen-cli query "What is the weather today?"
```

The terminal will get the model's reaction after you send the query.

Step 3: CLI Options

The CLI offers a few essential command choices for clients to undertake:

- -h, --help: To see CLI help data attempt -h amplify.
- -v, --version: Shows the form of the show or CLI instruments.
- -k, --api-key: Indicates the API key for verification.
- --config: You'll name your own configuration file after you run the method through this choice.

Example:

The qwen-cli device questions the show and returns its yield once you enter "Let me know almost the history of AI" and give your_api_key_here.

Step 4: Running Scripts via CLI

Your framework can run inquiries naturally by executing CLI commands with predefined inputs in content records. This setup makes a difference when performing large-scale operations or timed job executions.

3. Accessing the Model via Web UI

Clients who need to work with the Qwen 2.5-Max show in a user-friendly design environment can utilize the Internet UI to connected with it.

Step 1: Accessing the Web UI

You'll be able reach the Internet UI when Qwen 2.5-Max comes with this interface and get to it through your web browser. To get to the demonstrate begin it through accessible methods and open the net address:

- **Local Installation**: You'll get to the model at http: //localhost: 5000 through your nearby establishment.
- **Cloud/Production Installation**: When utilizing cloud administrations you wish to enter the URL made accessible by your supplier.

The Web UI typically includes:
- **Input Field**: Open a content box to enter your ask informational into the framework.
- **Submit Button**: The Submit Button sends the request to the machine for handling.

- **Response Area**: The show shows its comes about in the Reaction Range segment.

Step 2: Interacting with the Web UI

Just type your search terms into the text box before pressing the Submit button. Your search query will reach Qwen 2.5-Max through the Web UI which will show you its results instantly.

Example: Enter your request by typing this message: "What is the weather today?" After entering "What is the weather today?" your request returns the answer "The weather today is sunny with a high of 75°F." The day is sunny and temperatures reach 75°F.

Step 3: Advanced Features in Web UI

Web UIs of some systems let you access further complex functions:

- **Response Tuning**: Adjust model parameters like creativity, verbosity, or tone of the response.
- **Session History**: The system shows and controls all previous chats.

- **Export Options**: You can save all discussions or individual responses recorded in multiple output formats including PDF and text.

Step 4: Authentication via Web UI

Order is processed only after you type your API key or complete secure OAuth login. You can adjust these settings from the Web UI's settings or login area.

Summary of Access Methods

Method	Use Case	Interaction Type	Authentication
API	For integration with external systems or custom apps.	HTTP requests (POST, GET).	API key (if required).
CLI	For local development, automation, and script-based access.	Terminal-based commands.	API key or environment variables.
Web UI	For a user-friendly interface and	Graphical user interface	API key or login required.

	quick interactions.	(browser-based).	

Conclusion

Qwen 2.5-Max makes it possible to utilize the model through various methods that adapt to developers, administrators and users. These ways of access suit different requirements and personal choices of users. Effective use of Qwen 2.5-Max access options enables you to apply its advanced features across multiple applications.

CHAPTER THREE

MODEL SPECIFICATIONS

Architecture & Parameters of Qwen 2.5-Max

Qwen 2.5-Max employs an architecture which defines its central framework together with important parameters to enable processing of complex operations such as natural language understanding and real-time interaction and content generation skills. This section discusses Qwen 2.5-Max architecture fundamentals as well as the main features that control its operational efficiency and structural conduct.

1. Architecture Overview

Qwen 2.5-Max relies on Transformer-like architecture which develops into the main processing structure for modern language models starting from GPT to BERT alongside T5. Qwen 2.5-Max consists of fundamental architectural components and design decisions which have been listed below.

Transformer Architecture

- **Self-Attention Mechanism**:
    - o Th Qwen 2.5-Max actualizes self-attention methods from the Transformer design to

decide word pertinence for sentences. The demonstrate can handle all relevant data in sentences amid its reaction era.

- o Self-Attention components empower Qwen 2.5-Max to analyze broad content conditions in this way guaranteeing solid understanding of complex implications over long content fragments.

- **Encoder-Decoder Structure (For Some Tasks)**:
  - o Certain adjustments of Qwen 2.5-Max actualize encoder-decoder design since they handle interpretation or summarization assignments. Be that as it may, content completion and address replying errands regularly utilize decoder-only structures. A demonstrate with as it were a decoder structure can address assignments requiring content completion and reply questions.

- **Multi-Head Attention**:
  - o The model performs multi-head attention between multiple input sequence positions during its computational process. A higher number of pattern discernment capabilities

emerge from this addition to the model architecture.

Model Layers and Depth

- **Number of Layers**:
    - The number of layers based on configuration can reach between 12 up to 48 layers in Qwen 2.5-Max. Higher layer count in a model enables its ability to understand progressively abstract language patterns.

- **Feedforward Networks**:
    - The self-attention strategy taken after by feedforward neural systems exists in each layer of the framework. Such setup empowers viable dealing with of input arrangements whereas bringing out complex designs amid preparing.

- **Positional Encoding**:
    - Transformers require positional encodings since their engineering needs built-in requesting capacities and these encodings give position data to the show approximately word arrangement course of action.

Scalability and Parallelization

- **Distributed Training**:
    - The designers outlined Qwen 2.5-Max to utilize conveyed preparing capabilities that span over different GPU units or machine clusters. The show works on a huge scale which makes it competent of handling sizable sums of information whereas running complex computations viably.

- **Parallel Processing**:
    - Through its parallel preparing structure the demonstrate outranks conventional successive models since it works with various input groupings at the same time and quickens execution.

Parameter Sharing and Efficiency

- **Sparse Attention** (Optional):
    - Qwen 2.5-Max ought to consider actualizing inadequate consideration innovation to diminish computational necessities since this optimization improves execution without contrarily influencing precision.

38

- **Model Pruning** (Optional):
  - o Qwen 2.5-Max actualizes demonstrate pruning for certain arrangements or lighter forms by eradicating repetitive weights from neural arrange models in arrange to improve speed and diminish show measurement.

2. Model Parameters

Qwen 2.5-Max requires a few critical hyperparameters and show setup components to alter its execution nearby its behavioral capacities. The model's handling strategy beside its reaction era capabilities depend on these parameters whereas too empowering specialized errand adjustment.

Core Hyperparameters

1. **Number of Layers** (n_layers):
   - o Controls the depth of the model. A model gains better complex language processing skills through additional layers at the expense of increased computing needs.
   - o Example: 12 layers for smaller configurations, 48 layers for larger ones.
   - o

2. **Hidden Size** (n_hidden):
   o Refers to the number of hidden units in each layer. The capacity of the model to understand data patterns efficiently improves when the hidden size becomes larger because the model can detect more sophisticated linguistic patterns.
   o Example: The number of hidden units stands at 768 units for smaller models while extensive models need at least 2048 hidden units.

3. **Number of Attention Heads** (n_heads):
   o Every multi-head attention operation includes this parameter which determines the number of attention heads it can run. The model gains improved ability to discover various data relationships by receiving additional attention heads which enables it to examine different elements of the input.
   o Example: Model design includes 8 attention heads for smaller configurations and 16 or more for larger models.

4. **Feedforward Size** (n_ff):
   - o The size of the feedforward network within each Transformer layer. The size of hidden layer transformations depends on the feedforward size dimension in each layer.
   - o Example: 3072 units for smaller models, 8192 units for larger ones.

5. **Embedding Size** (n_emb):
   - o The utilization of word embeddings which represent input tokens defines the embedding size in the system. The usage of bigger embedding formats enables better representation of word details.
   - o Example: 512 dimensions for small models, 1024+ dimensions for larger models.

6. **Dropout Rate** (dropout_rate):
   - o During training the dropout parameter sets random sections of input data points to zero value through each forward pass as a method to minimize overfitting. The dropout rate usually exists between 0.1 to 0.3.
   - o Example: 0.1 for smaller models, 0.3 for larger models.
   - o

7. **Learning Rate** (lr):

   o During training the learning rate determines the dimensions of the optimizer steps that would be taken. Model performance along with convergence depends heavily on achieving its crucial elements. The Qwen 2.5-Max uses Optimizers Adam and AdamW which are standard in its training process.

   o Example: The learning rate ranges between 1e-5 to 1e-4 during fine-tuning and uses either warm-up decay schedules.

8. **Batch Size** (batch_size):

   o The model determines the number of sample inputs required to modify weight updates as part of training operations. The efficiency of computation increases with larger batch sizes though this improvement requires additional memory resources.

   o Example: 32, 64, 128 samples per batch.

9. **Sequence Length** (max_seq_len):

   o The model maintains a certain maximum boundary which determines the total sequence length it accepts during processing. Model training performance improves through longer sequences but such extensions require higher computational processing.

- o Example: The example for shorter tasks requires 512 tokens but longer tasks need at least 1024 tokens.

3. Special Features and Configurations

Fine-Tuning Parameters:

Qwen 2.5-Max requires parameter adjustment for particular use case implementations in specific industries because fine-tuning matters for adaptation success:

- **Learning Rate for Fine-Tuning**: Fine-tuning requires a smaller learning rate of 1e-5 or similar magnitude.
- **Dataset Size**: Specific task adaptation depends heavily on the size of the dataset used for fine-tuning.
- **Epochs**: During fine-tuning the number of training epochs controls the amount of weight updates for the model.

Temperature and Top-k Sampling (For Generation Tasks):

- **Temperature** (temperature):
  - o The temperature parameter builds up the degree of haphazardness found in content era. Software-based randomization gets to be more eccentric when the temperature esteem stands at 1.0 but gets to be more unsurprising when set to 0.7.
- **Top-k Sampling** (top_k):
  - o During the generation process top-k sampling limits the selection of potential candidates to the k most probable options to maintain coherent output diversity.
  - o Example: The model analyzes only fifty highest probability tokens during each step through using a value of Top-k = 50.
- **Top-p Sampling** (top_p):
  - o Core testing plays a part as the parameter that decides the build-up likelihood for selecting tokens. The token determination handle stops when the running likelihood surpasses the characterized edge p.

- o Example: A demonstrate chooses its following tokens from a confined space that contains higher likelihood components when Top-p = 0.9 is set.

4. Summary of Key Parameters

Parameter	Description	Typical Value
n_layers	Number of Transformer layers	12-48 layers
n_hidden	Size of hidden layers	768-2048 units
n_heads	Number of attention heads	8-16 heads
n_ff	Size of the feedforward network	3072-8192 units
n_emb	Size of word embeddings	512-1024 dimensions
dropout_rate	Dropout rate to prevent overfitting	0.1-0.3
learning_rate	Rate of model weight updates during training	1e-5 to 1e-4
batch_size	Number of input samples per batch	32-128 samples
max_seq_len	Maximum sequence	512-1024 tokens

	length for processing input text	

Conclusion

Qwen 2.5-Max builds its show design from Transformer components which incorporate self-attention at the side multi-head consideration and disseminated preparing forms that empower productive dialect handling at scale. The operational characteristics of Qwen 2.5-Max are indicated by distinctive numerical controlling components which shape its usefulness nearby execution results. Particular applications or arrangement scenarios require diverse parameters counting number of layers and show estimate as well as consideration heads. The usage of fine-tuning parameters nearby testing strategies boosts both the flexibility and exactness level which makes the demonstrate reasonable for viable utilize.

Supported Languages & Tasks in Qwen 2.5-Max

The broad usefulness of Qwen 2.5-Max permits clients to apply it in various normal dialect preparing applications due to its capacity to back different assignments over distinctive dialects. This area will talk about which dialects Qwen 2.5-Max underpins in conjunction with its capable errand execution.

1. Supported Languages

Qwen 2.5-Max offers content preparing capabilities in an broad collection of distinctive dialects. The demonstrate has a solid design which empowers it to handle thousands of dialects since it experienced preparing on gigantic multilingual datasets. These are the major dialect sorts that Qwen 2.5-Max underpins for application:

Major Supported Languages
- English
- Spanish
- French
- German
- Italian
- Portuguese
- Dutch
- Russian
- Chinese (Simplified and Traditional)
- Japanese
- Korean

- Arabic
- Hindi
- Turkish
- Polish
- Swedish
- Danish
- Norwegian
- Finnish
- Czech
- Greek
- Romanian
- Hungarian
- Thai
- Vietnamese
- Hebrew

Support for Low-Resource Languages

- Swahili
- Amharic
- Bengali
- Tamil
- Punjabi
- Malay
- Tagalog
- Uzbek

- Basque
- Catalan

Qwen 2.5-Max underpins multilingual handling of both resource-rich dialects as well as rare dialects in this way making it appropriate for worldwide and area-specific applications.

Cross-lingual Capabilities

Qwen 2.5-Max highlights a instrument that lets it trade dialect data so it can execute machine interpretation and cross-lingual data recovery capacities for dialects which have constrained preparing information.

2. Supported Tasks

Qwen 2.5-Max illustrates broad versatility since it works on different common dialect preparing (NLP) assignments. The most operational capabilities of Qwen 2.5-Max comprise of the taking after:

Text Generation

- **Creative Writing**: Create imaginative substance, such as stories, lyrics, and exchanges.

- **Content Creation**: The framework produces writings counting web journal substance and showcasing pieces and article pages.
- **Email Drafting**: Qwen 2.5-Max employments given enlightening to create programmed mail drafts.
- **Product Descriptions**: Create item depictions for e-commerce stages.

Text Understanding

- **Sentiment Analysis**: Classify the opinion of a given content (positive, negative, unbiased).
- **Emotion Recognition**: An API identifies feelings counting delight and outrage and pity and shock and others inside content records.
- **Text Summarization**:
  - **Extractive Summarization**: Content rundown creation includes extricating key substance areas which frame the premise of the outline.
  - **Abstractive Summarization**: The framework creates outlines which rethink unique content into abbreviated compositions.

- **Text Classification**: The framework employments content classification to partitioned writings between pre-defined categories for applications like spam location or news categorization.

Machine Translation

- **Language Translation**: Decipher content from one dialect to another. Utilizing Qwen 2.5-Max clients can perform interpretation between numerous distinctive dialect sets.
  - Example: Interpret from English to Spanish, French to English, or Chinese to Russian.

Question Answering

- **Fact-based Q&A**: The framework gives fact-based answers to express questions which relate to given composed substance.
- **Open-domain Q&A**: The demonstrate gives open-domain Q&A benefit which creates reactions for non specific questions from a endless assortment of points through its broad information database.
- **Closed-domain Q&A**: The framework offers closed-domain Q&A usefulness which gives arrangements interior specific information spaces

such as therapeutic and legitimate or monetary ranges.

Textual Entailment and Paraphrase Detection

- **Natural Language Inference (NLI)**: Natural Language Inference systems judge if the premise supports or opposes the hypothesis. Textual Entailment model helps us check for contradiction and factual accuracy plus support logical evaluations.
- **Paraphrase Detection**: The system finds out if two sentences keep the same message or if one sentence rephrases the other.

Named Entity Recognition (NER)

- **Entity Identification**: Our system detects and labels all specific words and names that appear in text documents.
- **Entity Linking**: When recognizing entities it matches them to a collection of organized knowledge items in a database (this links named entities to their Wikipedia profiles).

Text-to-Speech & Speech-to-Text (if applicable)

- **Text-to-Speech**: The application turns written material into spoken words. Such processing tools help develop chatbots that understand and interact with humans.

- **Speech-to-Text**: The system turns spoken words into text for users. The system needs this feature to work properly with programs that convert voice to text and aid users.

Dialogue & Conversational AI

- **Chatbots**: Construct chatbots that participate in normal and well-connected talks about different subject fields (such as customer help or educational experiences).

- **Multi-turn Conversations**: The software should handle multiple conversation exchanges while keeping all related parts.

- **Intent Detection**: The system understands users' needs when they send messages by detecting which action they want to perform.

Text Editing and Correction

- **Grammar & Spelling Correction**: The system automatically locates and fixes text spelling and grammar problems.

- **Paraphrasing**: The system automatically locates and fixes text spelling and grammar problems. Our system adjusts verbalization when it alters text flow to make content easier to understand.

- **Style Transfer**: Text style adjusting tool helps users change how written material looks through normalizing verbalization and tone selection.

Semantic Search & Information Retrieval

- **Search Engine Functionality**: Our search engine system finds and supplies appropriate documents paragraphs and answers from a big database based on user input.

- **Document Ranking**: The system produces document result lists that match user search needs based on their input requests.

Text-to-Image (if applicable)

- **Image Generation**: The framework can make pictures based on composed informational to serve imaginative and limited time ventures.

- **Image Captioning**: The show can make content clarifications from picture information when associated to a multimodal framework.

Code Generation and Assistance

- **Code Generation**: The AI framework turns expressive dialect into working program code.

- **Code Explanation**: The code portrayal framework depicts the work of each programming portion.

- **Code Debugging**: When code investigating happens this framework will discover absconds and propose arrangements.

3. Advanced Use Cases

Due to its progressed capabilities and wide parameter administration the Qwen 2.5-Max can adjust effectively to fulfill complex industry-specific assignments. The device handles complicated assignments such as those displayed underneath:

- **Healthcare**:
  - **Medical Text Classification**: Classify restorative records or inquire about papers into particular categories (e.g., infection conclusion, sedate adequacy).
  - **Clinical Question Answering**: The framework reacts to restorative request utilizing both clinical data and investigated discoveries.
- **Finance**:
  - **Sentiment Analysis for Financial News**: Our demonstrate makes a difference monetary experts see speculator sentiments toward showcase data from news articles and social nourishes.
  - **Risk Assessment**: Adam monetary archives to appear in case ventures and credits bring worthy dangers.
- **Legal**:
  - **Contract Review**: Consequently audit and highlight key areas or clauses in lawful reports.

- o **Legal Research**: Discover significant case laws, points of reference, or statutes in reaction to lawful questions.
- **Education**:
  - o **Tutoring Systems**: Give clarifications and help for understudies in subjects like math, science, and history.
  - o **Automatic Essay Grading**: The framework handles paper reviewing errands utilizing predefined assessment benchmarks to supply understudies with scored comes about and comments.

4. Summary of Supported Languages & Tasks

Supported Languages	Supported Tasks
English, Spanish, French, German, Italian, Portuguese, Chinese, Japanese, Korean, Russian, Arabic, Hindi, etc.	Text Generation, Sentiment Analysis, Machine Translation, Question Answering, Named Entity Recognition, Text Summarization, Paraphrase Detection, Dialogue Systems, Grammar Correction, and more.
Low-resource	Cross-lingual Tasks, Text

languages like Swahili, Amharic, Tamil, Punjabi	Classification, Sentiment Analysis, and more.

Conclusion

Qwen 2.5-Max works with multiple languages across a lot of natural language processing applications including text generation and translation plus emotion detection and chit chat functionalities. Its multilingual abilities help global companies while its broad task support helps different industries including healthcare financial services and learning systems.

CHAPTER FOUR

USAGE GUIDE

Basic Prompting Techniques for Qwen 2.5-Max

Using inputs properly remains the core requirement when you use Qwen 2.5-Max as a language model. Your prompt setup affects what the model generates in both quality and usefulness. This part explains standard prompt settings to produce top output from Qwen 2.5-Max.

1. Simple Text Generation

The simplest way to ask Qwen 2.5-Max for text output is through an open-ended input. Your choice of different prompts helps the model produce specific content types.

Example Prompts:

- **Creative Writing**: Describe the story of a dragon seeking to befriend a knight in his narrative.
- **Article/Blog Writing**: Display the positive aspects of solar energy through a 500-word paper.
- **Dialogue Generation**: The model should create dialogue between friends who make vacation plans.

Best Practices:

- Inform the writing model what mood you need the text to match. Tell us if you want to compose a humorous short story or an official email.

- To reach the right outcome specify added details about the content you want produced (project solar energy blogging for instance).

- If you need to display clear results apply separator marks such as direct quotes or bullet points when writing lists or dialogues.

2. Structured Prompts

Structured prompts let you guide the output results better. The prompts include detailed directions that show the model what to do and what factors to consider during output generation.

Example Prompts:

- **Instruction-based Text Generation**: Compose a formal message to your workmate that you must arrive late to the upcoming meeting. Be polite and concise.

- **Content with Parameters**: Create product descriptions of a new smartwatch system. The outline requires describing all three parts of a smartwatch including water resistance functionality heart-rate measurement and battery life that lasts 12 hours.

- **List Generation**: List five basic advantages of bringing reusable bags to do your shopping. Summarize each rational factor within your answer.

Best Practices:

- Give us both the task type (either list or essay) and the document style (dialogue if needed).
- Give the model clear limits including text lengths and theme preferences to refine its output results.
- To build organized tasks give your directions through easy-to-grasp small steps. The task requires you to develop a product description through three main sections: 1 2, and 3 Overview, 2. Key Features, 3.

3. Providing Context

The model shows better performance on context-based work when we give the context details to it upfront.

Example Prompts:

- **Question Answering**: Examine how the following text should be analyzed:

- **Passage**: In 1969 Neil Armstrong achieved the historic task of stepping onto the lunar surface for NASA during its Apollo 11 expedition.
- **Question**: The first human to take their feet on lunar soil belonged to whom?
- **Text Continuation**: The increasing storm made John run faster through the woods with his heart pounding.

Best Practices:
- Make all required context available within the assignment instructions. The technique helps most when working on question answering systems or text projects that need explanation or development.
- When giving different content segments continuously interface the assignment to the displayed section data.
- Be correct approximately what kind of unused advancement you need Qwen to make (for illustration "Total the story with a sensational bend").

4. Using Example-Based Prompts (Few-shot Learning)
Qwen 2.5-Max completes its work superior once you appear it case assignments through few-shot learning. The

demonstrate learns to recognize designs through the given tests at that point applies this information to handle errands taking after the illustrations.

Example Prompts:

- **Text Classification**: It would be ideal if you demonstrate in the event that these sentences are emphatically, adversely or impartially arranged:
    1. 'I love this movie, it's amazing!' → Positive
    2. 'The weather is terrible today.' → Negative
    3. 'I feel okay about this decision.' → Neutral
    4. 'I'm excited for the weekend!' → "

- **Text Summarization**: A inquire about group uncovered that ordinary physical movement makes individuals less focused and on edge around their mental well-being. Every day physical exercises like strolling biking and swimming cut back cortisol levels which researchers interface to push.

- **Code Generation**: Rethink this Python work to convert strings in switch arrange. Example:

- Input: 'Hello'
- Output: 'olleH'

Develop a work which tests whether a given number qualifies as prime.

Best Practices:

- Donate 2-3 test cases illustrating different sorts of input cases.

- State both the required input information structure and all required conclusion comes about.

- Rehash your chosen formatting for each illustration to assist the demonstrate see how the assignment must be done.

5. Conversational Prompts

Qwen 2.5-Max performs well at dealing with progressing exchanges and acing intelligently chatbot improvement. A clear talking way with adequate foundation makes a difference the framework deliver way better comes about.

Example Prompts:

- **Simple Conversation**: What does today bring weather-wise in Paris?

- **Interactive Q&A**: The user needs to know the basic steps to prepare coffee.

  Model: Begin by gathering coffee beans coffee maker and water.

  User: User wants to know which type of coffee beans to select.

- **Role-playing Dialogue**: Pretend you are a teacher. Teach photosynthesis basics to 5th-grade students in a simple way.

Best Practices:
- Make your conversation questions easy to understand.
- When there are several back and forth exchanges keep the model focused by returning to past discussion points.
- Decide how professional or casual your speech should be based on your application requirements.

6. Using Temperature and Top-k Parameters

You can use temperature and top-k settings of the model to achieve expert-level control when creating new responses.

Temperature:
- When your temperature setting reaches 1.0 it stimulates the model to produce varied imaginative results while reducing content creativity at 0.3.

Example with Temperature:

- o **High Temperature (creative)**: The model at high temperature needs you to create a poem about moonlight reflecting on calm ocean waters.

- o **Low Temperature (precise)**: The model will produce factual descriptions of how the moon affects the tide movements.

Top-k Sampling:

- The model chooses between multiple possible next words as specified through the top-k setting. Decreasing the top-k setting helps the system produce focused results while increasing it promotes output variety.

Example with Top-k:

- o **Top-k = 5 (focused)**: "Generate a list of five classic novels."

- o **Top-k = 50 (diverse)**: "Generate a list of creative gift ideas for a birthday."

Best Practices:

- Set temperatures for your model to affect creative output. For factual work set the value lower and raise it for creating new ideas.

- Change top-k value from smaller values to focus your outputs and larger values to discover multiple output options.

7. Avoiding Common Pitfalls

Standard testing of provoke tests depends on these fundamental rules:

- **Be specific**: Unclearness in your enlightening produces vague comes about. The quality of comes about moves forward after you donate more particular data to the framework.
- **Test iteratively**: Start with a beginning provoke and alter it concurring to the made yield amid testing. Your commands will create higher-quality comes about through this prepare.
- **Limit the scope**: When a errand region is as well broad the show needs more time and vitality to produce precise discoveries. Rethink your assignment when it gets to be as well wide for the show to handle.
- **Handle ambiguity**: When prompts have dubious implications include particular bearings or limits to them.

Conclusion

You need basic prompting methods to achieve successful results with Qwen 2.5-Max. When you create direct and precise task specifications the model will produce better results. The outlined techniques enable you to achieve better results from the model regardless of which features you want to test.

Advanced Features of Qwen 2.5-Max: Multi-turn Dialogue & Tool Usage

The new advanced features in Qwen 2.5-Max deliver many benefits by letting the model handle both lengthy conversations and work with external tools effectively. These advanced abilities allow the model to process multi-part discussions and access external tools to do more with its interactions. This section explains the advanced tools that Qwen 2.5-Max provides.

1. Multi-turn Dialogue

The model Qwen 2.5-Max can better respond to changing dialogues through multi-turn exchanges because it saves information between conversations. Creating these types of applications depends on this text processing feature.

Key Features of Multi-turn Dialogue:

- **Context Retention**: The model stores and recalls past conversation segments to engage in long-term multiple exchanges.

- **Dynamic Response Generation**: Our model updates its answers to match user demands by using existing discussion details.

- **Intent Detection**: When the model detects user intent it modifies its output to promote a realistic and enjoyable chat.

Example Interaction:

- **User**: The user wants to know about weather conditions today.

- **Model**: The model cannot access real-time data but will show you how to check the weather at your current location. Which major city are you looking to get information about?

- **User**: "New York."

- **Model**: Consumers in New York can discover current weather conditions through either Accu Weather or their smartphone weather apps for real-time information.

Best Practices for Multi-turn Dialogue:

- **Clarify User Intent**: When the model needs more detail about a user's question it must ask for better clues about their intention. When a user submits unclear information the model requests "Please give me more details about this." to gather more context.

- **Context Management**: During prolonged conversations when users give extensive details ensure that dialogue proves key references properly without introducing irrelevant information.

- **Turn-taking**: In multiple response situations arrange prompts to flow logically between turns of conversation. After responding to a query the model requests "Should we provide additional details?" I can assist you further if you need help.

2. Tool Usage

Through various applications programming interfaces Qwen 2.5-Max adds new functions beyond its basic features. This feature lets the model do practical work with real information and make decisions when it reads information from its user.

Types of Tools and Functions:

1. **API Integrations**:

    o **Search Engines**: Our framework interfaces to a look API to induce new substance from the web.

    o **Weather APIs**: Drag live climate information for distinctive areas in reaction to client inquiries.

    o **Currency Conversion**: The benefit appears current trade rates to change over monetary standards right away.

    o **News API**: Our News API can get each accessible news article and full substance from chosen themes.

    o **Flight Information**: Get to flight status, bookings, and carrier data.

2. **Code Execution**:

    o **Python Code**: We will run Python capacities without delay to perform scientific operations information examination or make programs with Qwen 2.5-Max. These assignments incorporate computer recreation models, data structure handling and visualizing data as charts.

3. **Custom Tools**:

   o You'll be able connect custom-made apparatuses specifically into your Qwen 2.5-Max app through extraordinary built programs based on your application counting item proposals or record administration.

Example of Tool Usage:

- **User**: "It would be ideal if you appear the London temperature perusing nowadays."
- **Model (with weather API integration)**: The temperature in London nowadays stands at 15 degrees Celsius.
- **User**: The client needs to know the Euro sum when trading 100 USD for euros.
- **Model (with currency conversion tool)**: Our benefit will transform that sum for you. [Calls money change API] The trade rate nowadays appears 100 US dollars matches 92 Euros.

Best Practices for Tool Usage:

- **Provide Clear Context**: Incorporate all apparatus informational clearly within the incite with particular errands laid out (such as change over 50 USD to GBP).

- **Limitations and Error Handling**: When an outside instrument cannot be gotten to or breaks the demonstrate has to react appropriately with articulations like "Something is wrong with the instrument right presently" or "The apparatus isn't working at this time if you don't mind attempt afterward".

- **Data Validation**: Test any inputs that go into our framework to affirm they coordinate device necessities and fit acknowledged parameters.

3. Using Multi-turn Dialogue with Tool Usage

Clients can associated with Qwen 2.5-Max through different discoursed whereas utilizing outside devices that require both spared setting and prepared information.

Example:

- **User**: The client inquires the framework to arrange a Paris trip.

- **Model**: I'd adore to assist! Would you would like help with getting Paris flight accessibility hotel listings or goal suggestions?
- **User**: "I'm fascinated by flights."
- **Model**: The demonstrate can help you with that assignment. What are the travel dates you arrange to utilize?
- **User**: The client needs flights from June 10th until June 20th.
- **Model (with flight tool integration)**: I will look at flight conceivable outcomes for those indicated dates whereas you hold up. If you don't mind hold on for a minute." [Calls flight booking API or web benefit] Amid the look I found multiple flight possibilities from Unused York to Paris. If you don't mind give which aircrafts you incline toward to see in conjunction with their cost ranges.

Best Practices for Multi-turn Dialogue with Tool Usage:
- **Seamless Transitions**: Effectively move between subjects when the subject gets to be flight booking. I can look for and recover the required data for you right presently.
- **Minimize User Input**: Diminish the number of steps clients have to be perform their errands. The

74

framework ought to offer proposed dates and fill in existing data when clients set up their dates of travel as this data matches their prior discourses.

- **Error Recovery**: The show should automatically offer replacement alternatives when API or device challenges happen furthermore it must inquire clients to alter their search criteria in case required.

4. Handling Complex Use Cases

The Qwen 2.5-Max system enables the execution of complex multi-step tasks which demand utilization of multiple external programs and comprehend diverse domains of information.

Example Use Case: Personalized Travel Assistant

1. **User**: The user requests to book a three-day visit to Paris using a travel budget of $1000. Can you help?"

2. **Model**: "Sure! You have my assistance to book flights while I will also find accommodations and pick activities according to your preferences. Let's start with flights. When do you want to depart?"

3. **User**: The user plans to depart on May 10th.

4. **Model (with flight tool integration)**: The model will review flight options between your present location and Paris for May 10th date.

5. **Model (after flight retrieval)**: The model displayed flights which were priced at $500. Hotels alongside activities will cost you the remaining $500 after purchasing flight tickets. Should I help you find suitable hotels at this time?

6. **User**: The user requests to view hotel accommodations which are situated near the Eiffel Tower.

7. **Model (with hotel API)**: The hotel API showed you numerous accommodation choices located in the vicinity of the Eiffel Tower while remaining affordable. Which type of accommodations would you choose between a 3-star hotel and a 4-star hotel?

8. **User**: The user requests to book a hotel rated at three star.

The system uses multi-turn dialogue together with tool integration tools for real-time flight and hotel data retrieval to deliver a seamless journey for users.

5. Advanced Customization and Integration

Qwen 2.5-Max serves complex applications by allowing development of custom tool integration with its capabilities. Developers can implement their own custom tool connections as well as:

- **CRM Systems**: CRM Systems enable users to search and change database records of customers.
- **E-commerce Platforms**: The platform provides two functionalities that include product recommendation based on user preferences along with inventory checking abilities.
- **Healthcare Systems**: Healthcare Systems enable database access to patient medical records and answers specific queries and provides recommendations through this system.

Custom Integration Example:
- **User**: The user inquiries about their current order status.
- **Model (with e-commerce integration)**: The system with e-commerce integration will verify your order status now. The system extracts order data from e-commerce platform Application Programming Interface (API). The order with

number #12345 remains under processing until shipment takes place tomorrow.

Conclusion

Qwen 2.5-Max's capacity to preserve multi-turn discoursed with instrument utilization bolsters engineers in making complex conversational specialists nearby chatbots as well as virtual collaborators. These built-in features enable the demonstrate to preserve intelligently discussions through setting mindfulness whereas it performs coordinates real-time information recovery and executes multistage complex assignments. The progressed highlights empower engineers to develop personalized interfacing that join together Qwen 2.5-Max's discussion capabilities with coordinates outside apparatus usefulness.

CHAPTER FIVE

API & INTEGRATION

API Endpoints & Authentication for Qwen 2.5-Max

The most advantage of working with Qwen 2.5-Max includes getting to its show through automatic API endpoints which give clients with programming interface get to. The endpoints implanted in Qwen 2.5-Max permit engineers to blend the show capabilities into their applications so they can perform errands such as producing writings and managing conversations along side extra functionalities. The get to necessities of these endpoints have to be combine confirming strategies for keeping up security. The taking after portion illustrates Qwen 2.5-Max's basic API focuses with their utilization informational and define confirmation steps for executing API demands.

1. API Authentication Overview

The engineering of API verification lets authorized clients make contact with and get to the Qwen 2.5-Max demonstrate capacities. API verification requires a method of authorization through API keys or OAuth tokens that are essential for each client ask.

Common Authentication Methods:

1. **API Key**:
   - **Description**: The system utilizes API keys as a one of a kind verification strategy which empowers clients to confirm API execution demands. These verification keys are transmitted through HTTP header segments or inquiry parameter areas.
   - **Example Header**: Authorization: Bearer <API_KEY>
   - Directors get to the comfort to allow clients API keys when they make or enroll accounts and they can moreover recover or disavow API keys through the support interface.

2. **OAuth 2.0**:
   - **Description**: OAuth 2.0 speaks to an progressed security convention and adaptable convention framework that empowers designated get to authorization. OAuth empowers clients to verify employing a third-party supplier for getting to Qwen 2.5-Max's administrations without exposing their account subtle elements to the application.

- **Example Flow**:
  - Clients can get to the framework through their OAuth supplier account some time recently moving forward.
  - The application has to get an OAuth token through its verification ask.
  - The API demands transmit verification token to confirm the demands.

Setting Up Authentication:

1. **Obtain API Key or OAuth Token**:
   - Clients must verify themselves with Qwen 2.5-Max stage through enlistment to obtain either an API key or an OAuth token.
2. **Include in Requests**:
   - Guarantee the API key or token integration happens either through ask header areas or inquiry parameter strategies amid API ask operations.

2. API Endpoints

Qwen 2.5-Max enables API get to to diverse usefulness that incorporates content era along side multi-turn discussions and outside apparatus usefulness.

Common API Endpoints:

1. **Text Generation Endpoint**

   o **Endpoint**: /v1/generate-text

   o **Method**: POST

   o **Description**: The endpoint empowers clients to make content substance from a given beginning content together with temperature control parameters. The framework will deliver an yield after analyzing the content you allow it.

   o **Request Body**:

   o {

   o The ask incorporates "incite" containing "Era of a healthcare AI web journal article" for the API to work. o "temperature":

   o "temperature": 0.7,

   o "max_tokens": 500

   o }

   o **Parameters**:

   ▪ prompt: The section point we offer for the era handle is known as provoke.

   ▪ temperature: Controls the arbitrariness of the yield. Higher values of 1 within the parameter will make more arbitrary writings but lower values of deliver centered content yield.

- max_tokens: The most extreme token constrain for the created reaction stands at max_tokens.

2. **Conversation Management Endpoint**

   o **Endpoint**: /v1/converse

   o **Method**: POST

   o **Description**: The endpoint carries on as a setting administration framework which permits Qwen 2.5-Max to perform multi-turn discussions by keeping up exchange systems and producing suitable reactions.

   o **Request Body**:

   o {

   o "session_id": "unique-session-id",

   o "message": The ask content contains the taking after input message "What is the capital of France?"

   o }

- o **Parameters**:
    - session_id: A one of a kind identifier for the discussion session. The framework employments this endpoint to track setting between different trades in sessions.
    - message: The user's current turn input message shows up in this parameter.

3. **Tool Integration Endpoint**
   - o **Endpoint**: /v1/tool-use
   - o **Method**: POST
   - o **Description**: This endpoint gives the demonstrate with an interface to get to coordinates apparatuses whether they are climate APIs or flight data.
   - o **Request Body**:
   - o {
   - o "tool_name": "weather_api",
   - o "parameters": {
   - o "city": "Paris"
   - o }
   - o }

- **Parameters**:
  - tool_name: The outside apparatus interatomic through tool_name which characterizes its title.
  - parameters: The particular parameters for the apparatus (e.g., city title for a climate device).

4. **Model Configuration Endpoint**
   - **Endpoint**: /v1/model-config
   - **Method**: GET
   - **Description**: This endpoint empowers clients to recover all dynamic setups of the Qwen 2.5-Max demonstrate beside its capabilities and flexible parameters and settings.
   - **Response**:
   - {
   - "model_name": "Qwen 2.5-Max",
   - "max_tokens": 4096,
   - "supported_languages": ["English", "Spanish", "French", "German"]
   - }

3. Example API Request

An case API ask to create content through the endpoint requires this sentence structure when verifying with an API key:

```
curl -X POST https://api.qwen.com/v1/generate-text \
    -H "Authorization: Bearer YOUR_API_KEY" \
    -H "Content-Type: application/json" \
    -d '{
        "prompt": The asked brief story depicts a cutting edge city,
        "temperature": 0.7,
        "max_tokens": 200
    }'
```

Request Breakdown:

- **URL**: https://api.qwen.com/v1/generate-text (the endpoint URL)
- **Authorization**: Carrier YOUR_API_KEY (supplant together with your real API key)
- **Headers**:
  - Content-Type: The ask body arrange employments application/json as its determination through Content-Type.

- **Body**: JSON information contains the incite and parameters (temperature and max_tokens) in its body section.

4. Error Handling and Rate Limiting

API endpoints commonly indicate rate limits that both ensure their frameworks and make reasonable openings for clients to utilize the administrations. The API will return such mistakes to clients who hit their rate restrain edge together with a particular blunder code.

Common Error Codes:

- **400 Bad Request**: The framework reacts with 400 Awful Ask when the ask organize or fundamental parameters are inaccurate.
- **401 Unauthorized**: The 401 Unauthorized reaction sends a notice around fizzled verification which might result from utilizing an invalid or truant API key.
- **429 Too Many Requests**: Rate limits have been surpassed since of the 429 As well Numerous Demands blunder. Hold up and retry after a indicated period.

- **500 Internal Server Error**: An startling server-based mistake comes about in a 500 Internal Server Error reaction message.

Handling Errors:

- Major blunders ought to be taken care of in your code through particular mistake administration methods to avoid framework breakdown. When experiencing a 429 As well Numerous Demands blunder you ought to apply a retry handle with an expanding delay time between endeavors.

5. Rate Limits & Usage Quotas

API suppliers utilize rate limits as a frame of manhandle avoidance and utilization control to characterize particular ask edges for one-minute or one-hour periods. Your utilization of the model's assets will be conveyed similarly among all clients since of this framework.

Example Rate Limiting:

- **Free Tier**: 100 requests per minute.
- **Premium Tier**: 1000 requests per minute.

A 429 as well Numerous Demands will show up once you break through the built up rate constrain. Checking your quantity utilization nearby creating error-recovery components ought to be your course of activity when rate constraining happens.

6. Security Considerations

Your framework has to take after security proposals whereas interfacing to Qwen 2.5-Max API:

- **Keep API Keys Confidential**: API keys must stay mystery by never uncovering them to open code stores or client-side JavaScript browser code. The server ought to keep up secure capacity of API keys.
- **Use HTTPS**: All demands must utilize the HTTPS convention to scramble transport of touchy data.
- **Regenerate API Keys**: You wish to use the API administration support to create an quick key substitution once you suspect an API key presentation.

Conclusion

The Qwen 2.5-Max API makes capable alternatives through its endpoints whereas providing strong verification capabilities for programmatically getting to the demonstrate. API key and OAuth token confirmation strategies along side appropriate understanding of all endpoints empowers you to create applications that completely utilize Qwen 2.5-Max capabilities. The integration handle needs secure execution with blunder dealing with and rate limit regard to convey smooth and secure intelligent.

Python SDK Examples for Qwen 2.5-Max

The Python SDK for Qwen 2.5-Max presents developers with an effortless way to interact with the model through its application programming interface. By using its SDK developers can swiftly connect Qwen 2.5-Max to their Python applications for executing text generation alongside multi-turn dialogue and tool instrument functions. Examples along with instructions provide a guide to work with Qwen 2.5-Max API through Python SDK.

1. Setting Up the Python SDK

Users must install the SDK as their first step before starting work with it. The Qwen 2.5-Max Python SDK installation becomes possible through pip if it is available for installation. You should run the command below to install it:

pip install qwen-sdk

Installation of the SDK requires a step where you must import its code base and authenticate through your API key.

2. Authentication with API Key

You need to authenticate through the Qwen 2.5-Max API using your obtained API key following the registration for access.

```
from qwen_sdk import QwenClient
# Initialize the QwenClient with your API key
client = QwenClient(api_key="your_api_key_here")
```

Through this client you can make all API requests directed at the Qwen 2.5-Max API.

3. Example 1: Text Generation

The example shows how users can use a basic prompt to obtain text creation results. The service allows response customization through adjustable attributes including temperature and max_tokens along with others.

```
# Define the text generation function
```

```python
def generate_text(prompt):
    response = client.generate_text(
        prompt=prompt,
        temperature=0.7,
        max_tokens=150
    )
    return response["text"]


# Example usage
prompt = The content requests writers to develop original storytelling regarding a teen girl discovering concealed territories.
generated_text = generate_text(prompt)
print("Generated Text: ", generated_text)
```

Explanation:

- **prompt**: The beginning text serves as the foundation for artificial intelligence generation.
- **temperature**: Controls the randomness of the response. Increasing the temperature setting on this scale produces results that are more creative or diverse in nature.
- **max_tokens**: max_tokens sets an upper boundary for word or fragment counts in generated results.

4. Example 2: Multi-turn Dialogue (Conversation Management)

As part of multi-turn communication the model maintains memory of previous messages to create appropriate answers. The example shows how to operate within a dialog sequence.

```python
# The function must define the practices for controlling
multi-turn dialogue.
def start_conversation():
    # Initialize the conversation session
    session_id = client.create_conversation()


    # The system will transmit your query afterward it
    delivers an appropriate answer.
    response = client.send_message(
        session_id=session_id,
        message="Hello, who are you?"
    )
    print("Model Response: ", response["text"])


    # Continue the conversation with a new message
    response = client.send_message(
        session_id=session_id,
        message="What can you do?"
```

```
)
print("Model Response: ", response["text"])

# Start the conversation
start_conversation()
```

Explanation:

- **create_conversation():**The function create_conversation initiates a new multi-turn session by preserving user context between multiple dialogue exchanges.
- **send_message():**The method send_message enables users to transmit messages which stay within the active dialogue session thus maintaining contextual understanding for improved responses.

5. Example 3: Tool Integration (Weather API)

The model applies with an external tool through an API to retrieve real-time data.

```
# The function retrieves the weather details by utilizing the tool through its interface.
def get_weather(city):
    # The tool retrieves weather data through its functionality.
```

94

```python
    response = client.use_tool(
        tool_name="weather_api",
        parameters={"city": city}
    )
    return response["weather"]


# Example usage
city = "Paris"
weather_info = get_weather(city)
print(f"The current weather in {city} is: {weather_info}")
```

Explanation:

- **use_tool():**The use_tool() function enables users to access integrated external tools for retrieving real-time data. A user must define both the tool name along with the required parameters that relate to the tool (here the city represents the weather parameter).

6. Example 4: Handling Errors

The application can respond in a controlled manner to failure situations including rate limiting and invalid inputs through proper error handling.

```python
# The function will generate text with built-in error
mitigation mechanisms.
def safe_generate_text(prompt):
    try:
        response = client.generate_text(
            prompt=prompt,
            temperature=0.7,
            max_tokens=150
        )
        return response["text"]
    except Exception as e:
        print(f"Error occurred: {e}")
        return None


# Example usage
prompt = The incite coordinates the AI framework to depict
the noteworthiness of AI innovation in restorative settings.
generated_text = safe_generate_text(prompt)
if generated_text:
    print("Generated Text: ", generated_text)
else:
    print("Failed to generate text.")
```

Explanation:

- **Error Handling**: The try-except square secures the program from mistakes counting arrange blunders and rate limits whereas showing valuable blunder messages to avoid program crashes.

7. Example 5: Customizing Model Parameters

Qwen 2.5-Max users can employ additional model parameters for specific adjustments of its output generation.

```
# The customized text generation function requires prompt
input alongside temperature and max_tokens parameters as
its inputs.
def customized_text_generation(prompt, temperature=0.7,
max_tokens=100):
    response = client.generate_text(
        prompt=prompt,
        temperature=temperature,
        max_tokens=max_tokens,
        top_p=0.9,  # controls the nucleus sampling
        frequency_penalty=0.5,  # reduces the frequency of
repeated phrases
        presence_penalty=0.3  # encourages new topics
```

```
)
return response["text"]
```

Example usage

```
prompt = The text needs to describe an advanced society
which controls all life aspects using technology at every
level.
generated_text  =  customized_text_generation(prompt,
temperature=0.8, max_tokens=200)
print("Generated Text: ", generated_text)
```

Explanation:

- **top_p**: The selection process based on probability distribution through nucleus sampling gives top_p the ability to generate more diverse text.

- **frequency_penalty and presence_penalty**: The model controls textual repetition with frequency_penalty whereas presence_penalty influences new topic introduction in the generated text.

8. Example 6: Model Configuration

The SDK provides you with model configuration functionality to obtain data about supported languages and model parameters.

```
# A function will retrieve the model configuration through the following code.
def get_model_config():
    config = client.get_model_config()
    return config


# Example usage
config = get_model_config()
print("Model Configuration: ", config)
```

Explanation:

- **get_model_config():**This command retrieves both the Qwen 2.5-Max model's present configuration together with its supported language options and its parameter settings.

Conclusion

The Python SDK for Qwen 2.5-Max creates a basic yet effective method to operate the model's API. The Python SDK of Qwen 2.5-Max provides development examples for multitudinous applications including text generation as well as multi-turn dialogue and tool usability and error resolution so developers can swiftly include Qwen 2.5-Max in their projects for different usages. Through its SDK the underlying complexities are pushed into the background so developers can build rich interactive systems without needing to manage API specifications.

CHAPTER SIX

FINE-TUNING & CUSTOMIZATION

Adapting Qwen 2.5-Max for Specific Tasks

Qwen 2.5-Max demonstrates high flexibility because developers can customize it to fulfill several uses including easy text generation together with sophisticated interaction models and analysis solutions. A person must learn methods for optimizing Qwen 2.5-Max to perform particular assignments by modifying the model for specific applications and applying training to unique resources while employing its sophisticated elements to generate precise results.

1. Task-Specific Fine-tuning (Transfer Learning)

The initial strength of Qwen 2.5-Max allows users to improve its capabilities further by tuning the model through specialized datasets for specific contexts. The process of fine-tuning makes the model learn domain-specific text which improves its capability to handle the particularities and context of that field.

Steps to Fine-tune Qwen 2.5-Max for a Specific Task:

1. **Prepare Your Dataset**: The first step entails gathering data which matches your desired use case

such that the model becomes expert in specific tasks. hayır 2.5-Max requires data about medical text so users who want medical text generation must gather medical literature and clinical documentation.

2. **Preprocessing**: Your dataset requires preliminary processing which should normalize its form according to the input specifications of the model. The processing work includes both making tokenization regular and handling specific tokens that the model expects.

3. **Fine-tuning**:

   o Projects that use fine-tuning include continuing pre-trained model learning sessions on specific datasets with transfer learning methods. The model parameters need adjustment to absorb registry-specific patterns that enhance its capability for performing the assigned task.

   o You can perform fine-tuning either through APIs or specialized platforms such as Hugging Face or a comparable tool which provides interfaces to execute training on custom datasets.

4. **Evaluate & Validate**: The validation set assessment should occur after model fine-tuning ends to check if the model performs acceptably on the exact task. You should modify the training settings to improve system performance.

5. **Deploy**: The deployment of your fine-tuned model should start when you reach satisfactory results through interfaces that support API endpoints or integrated applications or client interfaces.

2. Customizing for Specific Use Cases

You can make Qwen 2.5-Max work better for specific tasks through three methods: changing your model input prompt along with parameter adjustments and developing task-specific workflows. The model has several application-specific configurations which clients can use to customize their processes:

Example 1: Chatbots and Virtual Assistants

The conversion of Qwen 2.5-Max into a bot-based automated support system requires adjustments to focus on both dialog control systems and relevant response generation.

- **Use Case**: Customer support chatbot
- **Customization Approach**:
  - The model needs to use session-based memory technology to maintain knowledge about past dialogue interactions (multi-turn dialogues) for accurate context retrieval.
  - You should modify the prompts to address unique customer problems and solving methods.
  - Dynamic responses must use customer inputs while maintaining both the tone and relevant knowledge domain such as supplying product details together with step-by-step troubleshooting instructions.

```
# Example of a customer support chatbot
def customer_support_chatbot():
    session_id = client.create_conversation()
```

In the conversation the customer inquires about their order #12345 where service is provided during the conversation.

```
    response = client.send_message(session_id=session_id,
message=customer_message)
```

The customer sends customer_message "What's the status of my order #12345?" response =

```
client.send_message(session_id=session_id,
message=customer_message)                    print("Bot:",
response["text"])


    # Follow-up question
    follow_up = The user requests to modify shipping details
through the follow_up
    response = client.send_message(session_id=session_id,
message=follow_up)
    print("Bot:", response["text"])


# Start the chatbot interaction
customer_support_chatbot()
```

Example 2: Text Summarization

To generate summaries you should modify the model input by asking for a summary while defining max_tokens to achieve direct outputs.

- **Use Case**: In this use case the document or article needs to be transformed into a short summary.

- **Customization Approach**:
  - o Two short prompts for text summing up include "Summarize this text by relevant information points" and "Create an abbreviated version of the article.".
  - o The configuration includes adjusting max_tokens together with temperature to produce a suitable summary length while controlling creative output.

```
# Example of text summarization
def summarize_text(text):
    prompt = The following text requires a summary
according to the input document text.
    summary = client.generate_text(prompt=prompt,
max_tokens=100, temperature=0.3)
    return summary["text"]


# Example usage
text_to_summarize = The advanced Qwen 2.5-Max AI
model functions within natural language processing
applications to generate text along with answering
questions while completing text summaries.
summary = summarize_text(text_to_summarize)
print("Summary:", summary)
```

Example 3: Sentiment Analysis

Qwen 2.5-Max requires modification into a sentiment analysis system where it identifies or evaluates the emotions of written content.

- **Use Case**: Qwen 2.5-Max performs sentiment analysis tasks on customer feedback through its Use Case application.
- **Customization Approach**:
    - Change the model prompt into an instruction to detect sentiment orientation when provided with an input text.
    - You can proceed to analyze the model response then apply it to distinct sentiment categories which could include "Positive" "Negative" and "Neutral.".

```
# Example of sentiment analysis
def analyze_sentiment(text):
    prompt = The input text requires sentiment analysis to
determine its classification between positive and negative
and neutral sentiment.
    sentiment   =   client.generate_text(prompt=prompt,
max_tokens=50, temperature=0.5)
    return sentiment["text"]
```

```
# Example usage
customer_feedback = The new app version receives strong
praise from customers through their feedback which reads
"I love the new update to the app!". It's very user-friendly."
sentiment = analyze_sentiment(customer_feedback)
print("Sentiment:", sentiment)
```

3. Handling Domain-Specific Knowledge

The method of adjusting Qwen 2.5-Max for specialized
spaces counting law, pharmaceutical and innovation can be
progressed through providing domain-specific prompts
nearby related information. This hone empowers the model
to produce data that's particular to its space and exact to
genuine prerequisites.

Example: Legal Document Processing

Qwen 2.5-Max requires three steps to adjust for taking care
of lawful records through contract examination or inquire
about assignments:

1. **Use domain-specific prompts**: The show ought to
   get informational for investigation through

articulations such as "Look at the terms and conditions show in this contract."

2. **Feed specialized data**: Specialized information ought to be presented to the model through domain-specific legitimate archives which is able empower it to get it lawful phrasing and setting.

```
# Example of legal document processing
def process_legal_document(text):
    prompt = The input requires an examination of this legitimate record to extricate basic clauses which take after this literary substance:
    legal_analysis = client.generate_text(prompt=prompt, max_tokens=300, temperature=0.6)
    return legal_analysis["text"]


# Example usage
legal_text = The legal_text contains a State of California arrangement to set up its administration rules.
analysis = process_legal_document(legal_text)
print("Legal Analysis:", analysis)
```

4. Using Qwen 2.5-Max with External APIs and Tools

Qwen 2.5-Max offers capacity to associate with external APIs as well as existing instruments for errands that require live information recovery from third-party administrations. Qwen 2.5-Max empowers integration with various external APIs that incorporate climate data at the side flight benefit APIs and outside databases.

Example: Integrating with a Weather API

```
# Example of using Qwen 2.5-Max to integrate with a
weather API
def get_weather_for_city(city):
    prompt = f"Fetch the current weather for {city} from the
weather API."
    weather_info                                           =
client.use_tool(tool_name="weather_api",
parameters={"city": city})
    return weather_info["weather"]


# Example usage
city = "New York"
weather = get_weather_for_city(city)
print(f"Weather in {city}: {weather}")
```

Qwen 2.5-Max gets extended and energetic reaction information through this procedure by joining information from exterior sources.

5. Monitoring and Evaluation

You wish to preserve ceaseless observing and assessment of adjusted Qwen 2.5-Max after its particular errand execution to ensure exact and important yields. You ought to set up routine evaluation appraisals by testing demonstrate yield against predefined comes about along with client comments.

- **Metrics**: Utilizing measurements framework permits clients to track exactness nearby F1 score and BLEU score execution which are reasonable for assignments counting summarization or address replying.
- **User Feedback**: Real-time client input serves as an advancement instrument for the demonstrate through consistent provoking changes and unused information preparing sessions.

Conclusion

The customization prepare for Qwen 2.5-Max looks for changes in provoke input arrange whereas it gets fine-tuning treatment with specialized assignment information and interfaces to outside program interfacing and programming applications. With its progressed capabilities and adaptable design Qwen 2.5-Max can be personalized to perform different applications over individual discussion bots to rundown era and assumption handling and domain-based data recovery assignments.

CHAPTER SEVEN

PERFORMANCE OPTIMIZATION

Speed vs. Accuracy Trade-offs in Qwen 2.5-Max

Users of Qwen 2.5-Max need to determine the right ratio between response speed and output accuracy while using the model. An important consideration because performance adjustments to one factor will influence the other. Learning to adjust this endpoint relationship will reach either higher speed or enhanced accuracy according to what your input objective seeks.

The following section will analyze speed and accuracy factors followed by optimization methods for parameters and eventual examples of speed-accuracy trade-offs in scenarios.

1. Factors Influencing Speed and Accuracy

Qwen 2.5-Max produces results according to multiple factors which determine its speed and accuracy performance:

a. Model Parameters:

- **Temperature**: Affects the randomness of the model's responses. Using an elevated temperature value at 0.8 generates elaborate and varied outputs that need extended processing time and reduced precision accuracy. When temperature setting is at 0.2 the system produces more precise and accurate outcomes but introduces restricted output range.
  - o **Trade-off**: During sampling at lower temperatures the model delivers more accurate results but loses its creative capacity while at higher temperatures the model becomes more random which creates computational delays through increased output complexity.
- **Max Tokens**: Token generation length depends on the Max Tokens setting. The generation process needs additional computational power and longer duration for longer responses.
  - o **Trade-off**: The accuracy of summarizing or providing comprehensive output increases with max_tokens at the cost of extended generation time.

- **Top-p (Nucleus Sampling)**: The diversity of text output is managed by Top-p (Nucleus Sampling). Higher values within the model control allow it to examine multiple options when selecting tokens which extends response durations yet produces more sophisticated accurate results.
  - o **Trade-off**: When using top-p values set at 0.7 runtime performance increases because the model gets fewer options to consider but the generated output becomes less sophisticated. A higher value (e.g., 0.9) produces more accurate, diverse, and creative responses but at the cost of additional processing time.
- **Frequency & Presence Penalties**: The two parameters regulate the model's reaction to repetitive content and changes of topic direction during the generation process.
  - o **Trade-off**: Using high values for frequency and presence penalties reduces repetitive responses while promoting diverse meaningful answers thus leading to more accurate dialogue models in extensive conversations or when avoiding redundant

statements. This adjustment process which recalculates possible response rankings causes a minor delay in the response generation speed.

b. Hardware & Infrastructure:

- Both speed and accuracy of Qwen 2.5-Max operations depend heavily on the hardware system where it operates. Using stronger GPU hardware instead of CPUs enables both faster model inferences and enables running complex procedures for maintaining accuracy.
  - o **Trade-off**: When working with restricted hardware such as CPUs users should decrease max_tokens and top_p parameters to keep response times reasonable even though this may produce slightly lower quality outputs.

c. Batch Processing:

- Putting several API requests into single batches allows possible system optimizations which minimize request overheads thus increasing processing speed.

- o **Trade-off**: Using batch processing to process multiple queries leads to a small reduction in response accuracy because resources need to be shared across different queries.

2. Optimizing for Speed or Accuracy
When to Prioritize Speed:

When immediate fast responses are crucial for system performance you should set speed as your main priority instead of focusing on accuracy in high-frequency systems and minimal-time chatbots and real-time applications (for example gaming customer service).

To optimize for speed:

1. **Lower Temperature**: Reduce the randomness of the output. Reducing complexity in response generation makes the model produce more direct outputs while also simplifying the process to generate various answers.

2. **Limit Max Tokens**: The restriction of max_tokens length through configuration improves response

time because it limits the total number of generated tokens.

3. **Reduce Sampling Size**: Reductions in top_p sampling values can limit the available token choices for the model to improve its response speed.

4. **Optimize Hardware Usage**: Environment performance gets improved through GPU adoption because GPUs perform model inference tasks with higher efficiency compared to CPUs.

5. **Simplify Tasks**: The model demonstrates faster performance when performing direct factual tasks and simple commands instead of open-ended multi-step problem-solving operations.

Example

```
# Optimizing for speed
response = client.generate_text(
    prompt=" The user query requests identification of the French capital city.
    temperature=0.2,   # Lower randomness for fast and deterministic answers
    max_tokens=50,   # Shorter answer
```

```
    top_p=0.7        # The response time will improve with
this top_p parameter value set at 0.7.
)
print(response["text"])
```

When to Prioritize Accuracy:

You should choose model accuracy over speed because the output quality matters most in technical writings and legal or medical writing and detailed customer service situations.

To optimize for accuracy:

1. **Increase Temperature**: A higher model temperature in your processing allows expanded output diversity that often produces more suitable results particularly when dealing with complex or open-ended assignments.

2. **Increase Max Tokens**: The maximum token length setting should be boosted so the model creates extended and carefully detailed responses.

3. **Higher Top-p**: By increasing the value of top_p the model receives more sampling flexibility which produces better results but slows down its speed.

4. **Enable Presence/Frequency Penalties**: A setting of higher presence along with frequency penalties enables systems to produce more detailed and

coherent answers and discourage repetitive patterns in extended dialogues or texts.

Example:

```
# Optimizing for accuracy
response = client.generate_text(
    prompt="Explain the theory of relativity in detail.",
    temperature=0.7,     # More diverse and accurate explanation
    max_tokens=400,   # Longer response for more detail
    top_p=0.9,       # Increased diversity for a richer output
    frequency_penalty=0.5,  # Reduces redundancy
    presence_penalty=0.5    # Encourages new and relevant content
)
print(response["text"])
```

3. Balancing Speed and Accuracy

Many applications that work with large systems or serve customers need to achieve optimal performance through combining fast response times and precise results. The process of parameter adjustment depends on the current situation to deliver optimal results:

1. **Real-time vs. Non-Real-Time**:
   o Real-time applications require precision that justifies extended periods of waiting although non-real-time applications which generate lengthy reports need accuracy first and ample waiting time is acceptable.
   o When operating chatbots or providing instant customer service the system must prioritize performance over precision because immediate responses take precedence.

2. **Dynamic Tuning**:
   o The context of each task whether for answering questions or creative writing tasks enables readers to modify control parameters automatically. The speed optimization setting should be used when addressing factual questions while accuracy become the primary focus when asked for creative writing or deep analysis.

3. **User Feedback Loop**:
   o The integration of user feedback systems enables you to determine how Trade-offs will be positioned in system development.

The optimization choice should aim for fast responses because your user base prioritizes quick solutions. Users who require comprehensive answers should use models configured for maximum accuracy because speed becomes less important to them.

4. Best Practices for Managing Speed vs. Accuracy

- **Profile Your Use Case**: Creating a profile of your use case requires you to precisely determine application requirements between real-time engagement and extensive analysis activities so you can modify model settings appropriately.

- **Monitor Performance**: Production monitoring must focus on latency speed and accuracy and relevance quality of the system responses while performing continuous assessments. Monitoring performance and adjusting parameters should take place when delays or accuracy declines occur within the system.

- **Adjust On-demand**: Your system should modify performance parameters either through individual requests or through current system workload in order to find equilibrium between user demands and resource use.

Conclusion

The key requirement for working with Qwen 2.5-Max is the proper management of speed and accuracy between each other. To match your application requirements you might need to modify configuration settings such as temperature and both max_tokens and top_p values until you reach the optimal performance. Speed takes precedence for live operations yet select accuracy as the essential factor when aiming for exact and sophisticated high-quality results. The optimization of Qwen 2.5-Max depends on your specific requirements through proper adjustment of system settings and performance observation.

Hardware Recommendations for Qwen 2.5-Max

The choice of hardware plays a critical role for Qwen 2.5-Max deployment because it affects system performance when processing large models and providing real-time feedback. Using appropriate hardware leads to significant improvements in system response time and model accuracy as well as operational system performance.

This chapter provides essential hardware guidance for Qwen 2.5-Max deployment across various circumstances such as server operation within local premises and cloud infrastructure together with edge devices.

1. General Hardware Requirements
a. CPU vs. GPU

- **CPU (Central Processing Unit)**: Running Qwen 2.5-Max on CPUs remains possible while CPUs prove considerably slower than GPUs when operating large-scale language models since CPUs lack optimized parallel capabilities needed for deep learning operations. A CPU can operate Qwen 2.5-Max for testing small-scale applications or development purposes although it lacks the capacity to preserve production performance at scale.

- **GPU (Graphics Processing Unit)**: The optimal solution for text generation tasks together with heavy request processing demands relies on GPU (Graphics Processing Unit hardware. Operation of deep learning and machine learning models requires GPU hardware built to execute parallel processing operations. The processing speed of GPUs surpasses CPUs when executing matrix multiplications representing the core operations in neural network analyses.

b. Memory (RAM and VRAM)

- **RAM (Random Access Memory)**: Qwen 2.5-Max requires adequate Arbitrary Get to Memory (Slam) back which depends on show measurement and operational complexity. The suggested memory prerequisite for Qwen 2.5-Max incorporates at slightest 32GB of Irregular Get to MEMORY particularly amid operations with enormous models and long text-based induction errands.
  - o **For smaller-scale use cases**: The prerequisites for smaller-scale applications run between 16GB to 32GB of Smash.
  - o **For large-scale inference and fine-tuning**: When performing broad deduction errands at the side fine-tuning operations a framework requires at slightest 64GB of Slam or more.
- **VRAM (Video RAM)**: The VRAM necessity (Video Smash) gets to be fundamental when working the demonstrate through a GPU since it decides its execution capability. A adequate sum of Video Slam (VRAM) is basic for Qwen 2.5-Max

operations since its huge show measure makes memory bottlenecks which influence show deduction effectiveness.

- ○ **Minimum VRAM**: 16GB VRAM for smooth operation with bigger models.
- ○ **Recommended VRAM**: 24GB VRAM (e.g., NVIDIA A100, RTX 3090) for dealing with complex workloads without performance corruption.

2. Recommended GPUs

The foremost successful GPUs which work well for Qwen 2.5-Max-sized AI models incorporate these essential cases:

a. High-end GPUs (For Large-Scale, High-Performance Applications):

These GPUs give greatest execution in production-level situations which prepare different synchronous deduction demands as well as preparing and fine-tuning operations.

- **NVIDIA A100** (40GB/80GB VRAM): Clients running Qwen 2.5-Max advantage from the NVIDIA A100 GPU since of its tall execution together with 40GB or 80GB of VRAM for handling expansive models successfully.

126

- **NVIDIA V100** (16GB/32GB VRAM): The NVIDIA V100 GPU with either 16GB or 32GB VRAM belongs to a high-performance category which viably underpins machine learning operations.

- **NVIDIA RTX 3090** (24GB VRAM): The RTX 3090 by NVIDIA performs Qwen 2.5-Max induction errands viably and remains reasonable whereas giving 24GB of VRAM memory capacity.

b. Mid-range GPUs (For Moderate-scale Applications): These GPUs work well once you require direct execution capabilities together with budget-friendly needs for applications such as small-scale deduction operations and advancement needs.

- **NVIDIA RTX 3080** (10GB/12GB VRAM): Developers who prioritize both performance and reasonable costs should consider the NVIDIA RTX 3080 model with an option between 10GB and 12GB of VRAM.

- **NVIDIA RTX 3070** (8GB VRAM): A developer requiring cost-effective lower-volume inference capabilities should consider the NVIDIA RTX 3070 (8GB VRAM) GPU for its performance even though its response times will be slower than elite-level systems.

- **NVIDIA Tesla T4** (16GB VRAM): Ideal for cloud-based or smaller-scale deployments.

c. Budget GPUs (For Small-Scale or Testing Environments):

These graphics processing units will work well for people who have constrained resources or who want to evaluate their model construct on a reduced platform.

- **NVIDIA RTX 2060/2070/2080** (6GB-8GB VRAM): Qwen 2.5-Max operates on models with small data requirements when powered by NVIDIA RTX 2060/2070/2080 GPUs which have 6GB to 8GB of VRAM memory although these GPUs are not appropriate for commercial use.
- **NVIDIA GTX 1080 Ti** (11GB VRAM): A solid choice for smaller, lower-budget setups for testing and development.

3. Cloud-Based Hardware for Scalable Deployment

Many organizations along with developers seeking application expansion find cloud-based solutions provide them with the most efficient solution. Qwen 2.5-Max requires substantial processing power but cloud providers give customers access to elastic computing capabilities that eliminate the need for purchasing expensive physical hardware.

a. Cloud Service Providers

- **Amazon Web Services (AWS)**: The cloud service provider Amazon Web Services delivers potent computing instances for AI and machine learning operations through their p4d instances with A100 GPUs and p3 instances with V100 GPUs as well as g4dn instances containing T4 GPUs. High-performance workloads demand these instances as their optimal solution.

- **Google Cloud Platform (GCP)**: The Google Cloud Platform provides users access to three key GPU devices which include A100 and V100 and TPUs (Tensor Processing Units) ready for extensive deep learning operations. GCP enables users to alter their instance capability according to their current requirements.

- **Microsoft Azure**: Microsoft Azure produces deep learning workloads and model inference capabilities through its N-Series VMs NCv3 and NDv2 which provide GPU access with Tesla V100 and NVIDIA A100 and T4 models.

- **IBM Cloud**: The IBM Cloud platform provides GPU-powered computing capabilities which grant users Tesla V100 and NVIDIA A100 GPU access for both model training together with inference.

b. On-Demand and Spot Instances:

- Most cloud providers include spot instances or preemptible VMs that deliver significant cost discounts yet they can be interrupted. These workloads which do not need immediate processing such as batch processing or Qwen 2.5-Max training find appropriate solutions in on-demand allocations.

4. Network Considerations

Performance suffers substantially when large applications run in cloud environments or across multiple nodes unless network speed and bandwidth receive sufficient attention.

- **Low Latency**: Real-time applications needing interactions that require immediate responses must have low-latency networking setup. Distributed and multiple GPU setups need this particular feature to function effectively.

- **High Bandwidth**: The transfer of large data assets calls for high-bandwidth networking which needs to be set at 10Gbps or greater parameters especially if you use multiple instances for model fine-tuning tasks.

5. Storage Recommendations

Storage needs differ according to the specific application that you operate. The process of model checkpoint handling alongside data storage and logging needs access to fast storage systems that scale smoothly.

- **SSD (Solid-State Drive)**: The Solid-State Drive (SSD) establishes itself as necessary equipment due to its capability to manage data at elevated speeds during write and read sessions. The highest possible data throughput during active training and production systems comes from using NVMe SSDs.
- **Distributed File System**: Distributed File Systems should be employed for large datasets alongside multiple machines using solutions that include Amazon S3 and Google Cloud Storage or distributed file systems like Ceph or HDFS.

6. Power Supply & Cooling

Adequate power supply management combined with cooling solutions stands essential for high-end GPU performance stability and to avoid hardware failure.

- **Power Supply**: Your control supply framework ought to be competent of overseeing the critical electrical requests of server hardware beside GPU devices. Numerous GPU servers require two free control supplies to realize framework solidness.

- **Cooling Solutions**: Legitimate cooling through either fluid or discuss ought to be implemented to avoid issues when running resource-intensive models such as Qwen 2.5-Max. Appropriate wind stream in conjunction with cooling capacities ensure equipment from harm and overheating.

7. Edge Devices and Lightweight Models

Qwen 2.5-Max requires substantial resources which makes it inappropriate for deployment on mobile phones and IoT devices. Small versions of the model as well as model distillation let developers generate lightweight versions for implementation on basic hardware platforms.

- **Edge AI Hardware**: Edgeworks utilizing NVIDIA Jetson (TX2, Xavier) alongside Google Coral platform perform AI-based inference operations through their dedicated AI-specific hardware yet these devices demonstrate reduced processing capabilities in comparison to specialized GPUs.

- **Model Distillation**: Model Distillation should be applied to Qwen 2.5-Max for reducing its size and resource requirements while maintaining good performance when deploying to edge devices.

Conclusion

Deciding on appropriate hardware selection matters fundamentally for Qwen 2.5-Max deployment because it directly influences the system performance according to particular use requirements. The NVIDIA A100, V100, and RTX series along with GPUs are suggested for large-scale inference and training operations but CPUs work for more compact testing needs and smaller-scale operations. The deployment of cloud solutions relies on A100 and V100 and T4 GPU instances to manage scalability alongside cost-effectiveness. You should equip the model with appropriate memory additions of RAM and VRAM and rapid storage solutions for optimal performance.

The deployment process requires proper network planning as well as cooling engineering to achieve continuous dependable system performance.

CHAPTER EIGHT

TROUBLESHOOTING & FAQS

Common Issues & Solutions for Qwen 2.5-Max

Clients working with Qwen 2.5-Max have to be bargain with different stage issues that incorporate sending issues and execution bottlenecks as well as wrong yield comes about. The taking after segment contains a list of common issues with their comparing arrangement strategies.

1. Slow Response Times

Issue: Qwen 2.5-Max some of the time falls flat to reply rapidly whereas making deductions and when preparing an intemperate number of concurrent demands.

Possible Causes:

- **High model complexity**: The complexity of huge models causes Qwen 2.5-Max to require longer terms to deliver its reactions.
- **Insufficient hardware resources**: The system's capability to perform induction will be moderated down in case it has inadequately equipment assets counting CPU and GPU.

- **Suboptimal parameters**: The reaction time increases when creating different yields since tall values for temperature and max_tokens in conjunction with top_p lead to more complicated reaction era.

Solutions:

1. **Optimize Model Parameters**:
   - The reaction time makes strides when bringing down the temperature parameter since it diminishes reaction haphazardness.
   - To abbreviate the reaction time the max_tokens esteem needs lessening since shorter yields produce speedier era speeds.
   - The inspecting prepare will gotten to be quicker by diminishing top_p to 0.7.

2. **Upgrade Hardware**:
   - The deduction time will diminish essentially after you supplant a CPU with GPU gadgets such as the NVIDIA A100 or RTX 3090 which have plentiful accessible VRAM.
   - For productive demonstrate execution both Slam and GPU VRAM ought to be set at slightest 32GB Smash and at slightest 16GB for greatest VRAM.

3. **Use Batch Processing**:
   - Operations requiring numerous API demands ought to execute group handling to improve both handling speed and cut down on API administration costs.

4. **Leverage Cloud-based Solutions**:
   - Your organization ought to utilize cloud administrations from AWS along side Google Cloud and Sky blue since these offer flexible GPU occasion execution capabilities.

2. Memory Errors or Out of Memory (OOM) Issues

Issue: Understudies frequently run into "out of memory" framework blunders when performing deduction or preparing that happens primarily due to the combination of sizable models nearby substandard computing gear.

Possible Causes:
- **Model size**: The expansive measure of Qwen 2.5-Max demonstrate requires gadgets to have adequate VRAM and Slam memory to maintain a strategic distance from memory-related blunders.
- **Large input sequences**: Such expansive input groupings which outperform the demonstrate token

confinements can trigger memory assignment disappointment within the framework.

- **Too many concurrent requests**: Numerous demands that at the same time run whereas surpassing memory capacity will over-burden the framework.

Solutions:

1. **Reduce Input Size**:
   - The show needs inputs broken down into lesser parts that can be handled one after another.
   - The max_tokens parameter ought to be set to a lower esteem to shrivel the created content yield.

2. **Use Model Quantization or Distillation**:
   - The demonstrate estimate gets to be essentially littler through quantization since it performs math operations at lower precision such as FP16 rather than FP32 which decreases memory utilization.
   - The method of demonstrate refining permits the era of Qwen 2.5-Max memory forms that keep up precision levels whereas requiring less framework assets.

3. **Switch to More Powerful Hardware**:

   - You ought to confirm that your GPU has at slightest 16GB of VRAM capacity since that sum will suffice for your work. Türk workers who utilize cloud-based occasions ought to select GPU arrangements including A100 or V100 gadgets since they offer prevalent memory capacities.

   - Including more framework Slam will empower effective execution of expansive demonstrate computations and guarantee the framework maintains a strategic distance from memory exhaustion issues.

4. **Scale Horizontally**:

   - The conveyed form of Qwen 2.5-Max needs appropriate setup where the demonstrate parts over different GPUs or machines to spread memory utilization.

3. Inaccurate or Unreliable Outputs

Chosen reactions from the demonstrate can be unreasonable or truthfully off base nearby being unessential.

Possible Causes:

- **High randomness settings**: Higher esteem settings related to arbitrariness will make imaginative yields that exist past truthful precision.

- **Input-related issues**: Unimportant or wrong comes about happen when the input prompts don't have appropriate structure.

- **Model limitations**: The yield comes about from Qwen 2.5-Max may not provide outright precision since it operates as a huge dialect show nearby other models that battle to supply outright exactness for complex specialized inquiries.

Solutions:

1. **Optimize Temperature and Sampling Parameters**:

   o The system response accuracy improves when you set the temperature parameter at 0.2 while lowering the sampling values.

   o You should decrease the value of top_to 0.7 to restrict potential token choices which helps the model become more accurate.

2. **Improve Prompt Engineering**:
   - The input prompt needs to contain an organized structure which also includes simplicity and directness. Choose queries that avoid confusing meanings along with those that are not too general.
   - You should provide context along with clear task guidelines for the model to generate accurate responses.

3. **Use Post-Processing**:
   - A cross-check filter system against specific databases or known information sources should be incorporated as a post-processing step to verify factual accuracy of model output.
   - You can enhance accuracy within certain applications through addition of retrieval-augmented generation (RAG) layers which bring in knowledge from external sources.

4. **Model Fine-tuning**:
   - You should fine-tune your model with specialized data from your application domain when possible since doing so will

improve both response quality and relevance.

4. Model Not Generating Output or Timing Out

Issue: Users experience two problems with Qwen 2.5-Max: the model generates no output and sometimes takes too long during predictive operations.

Possible Causes:

- **API rate limits**: High-volume API traffic combined with many requests leads to service throttling or API rate limit restrictions.

- **Insufficient resources**: Your machine lacks capability to process computational tasks associated with the model functions.

- **Connectivity issues**: Connectivity issues occur when you use cloud-based APIs or services because network problems lead to service communication delays or failures.

Solutions:

1. **Check API Rate Limits**:
   - Cloud-based API users should determine if rate limits exist in their current usage. Most providers let users track usage levels but

offer expanded ability to increase service amounts through their higher plan subscriptions.

- o Your application requires a built-in retry system so it can respond to occasional occurrence of timeouts and rate-limiting problems.

2. **Optimize Resource Allocation**:

- o The equipment framework or cloud occasion needs adequate CPU at the side GPU and memory to function Qwen 2.5-Max viably.

- o Cloud occasion choice requires assets that coordinate the specified workload control so you ought to choose an NVIDIA A100 for seriously operations.

3. **Improve Network Connectivity**:

- o You ought to keep up reliable organize associations since the show exists in farther areas and this influences execution. For crucial applications utilize quick associations and neighborhood information centers as essential facilitating areas.

o Check for benefit disturbances which influence execution in the event that you work from a cloud-based framework.

5. Model Overfitting (During Fine-Tuning)

Issue: When performing Qwen 2.5-Max fine-tuning you might encounter demonstrate overfitting which leads to great comes about on preparing information but destitute execution on modern information tests.

Possible Causes:

- **Insufficient training data**: When performing Qwen 2.5-Max fine-tuning you might encounter demonstrate overfitting which leads to great comes about on preparing information but destitute execution on modern information tests.
- **Too many epochs**: Running the show for more ages than fundamental leads to specialization of the demonstrate with its preparing information.

Solutions:

1. **Data Augmentation**:
   o Your preparing information must incorporate different tests which speak to real-world scenarios to extend its

144

differences. The dataset extension empowers way better generalization of the demonstrate.

2. **Early Stopping**:

   o Early ceasing ought to be applied during fine-tuning to piece overfitting from happening. Halt the preparing handle when validation loss comes to a level or falls apart.

3. **Regularization Techniques**:

   o The expansion of dropout or weight rot regularization methods ought to be utilized to halt the show from overfitting amid preparing sessions.

4. **Cross-validation**:

   o Show execution appraisal utilizing cross-validation ought to span distinctive parts of the information to avoid overfitting when learning from a single set.

6. Model Doesn't Respond as Expected in Multi-turn Dialogue

Issue: Qwen 2.5-Max empowers a multi-turn discourse but sometimes loses track of progressing discoursed or produces incomprehensible discussions amid expanded discourse.

Possible Causes:

- **Lack of proper context**: A model requires complete context of multi-turn conversations to properly understand every exchange therefore previous exchanges need to be passed as context.
- **Token limits**: The model loses earlier context when conversations surpass its set token limit.

Solutions:

1. **Maintain Conversation Context**:
   - Each submission needs to include all preceding messages to retain full understanding of the dialogue. The entire conversation history should be added at the end of each input prompt to preserve context.
2. **Optimize Token Usage**:
   - A systematic strategy of trimming conversation texts and applying sliding context views helps the system provide relevant context to the model while staying under token constraints.

3. **Use Memory-augmented Techniques**:

   o To manage lengthy conversations the system requires retrieval-augmented generation (RAG) or external memory systems that help store and access past dialog data.

Conclusion

Users face typical problems when working with Qwen 2.5-Max although this model demonstrates high power as a language system. Most problems related to Qwen 2.5-Max usage can be resolved by optimizing model parameters along with sufficient hardware resources and better prompt design and best practices which include both fine-tuning and early stopping procedures. Cloud-based solutions with batch processing capabilities provide your application with efficient scalability when handling complex resource-heavy deployments. Addressing the usual problems before Qwen 2.5-Max implementation will enable successful and optimal system performance.

CHAPTER NINE

ETHICS & SAFETY

Responsible AI Guidelines for Qwen 2.5-Max

Artificial intelligence development requires immediate attention to ethical responsibility oversight. Qwen 2.5-Max functions like similar complex language models with strong features though it requires users to address questions about fairness together with transparency together with ethical accountability. Implementing responsible AI practices remains vital because it helps to minimize damage from AI systems as well as reduce unfair biases and counteract possible abuses when utilized for maximum AI technology advantages.

Guidelines for using Qwen 2.5-Max according to responsible AI principles will be detailed in this section with separate explanations on ethics and fairness and a discussion of transparency and privacy alongside an explanation of accountability.

1. Fairness & Bias Mitigation
a. Recognizing and Reducing Bias

Qwen 2.5-Max receives training input from enormous datasets which occasionally exhibit unbalanced or biased presentations of different population sectors alongside gender and ethnic groups. Different biases in Qwen 2.5-Max training create output results that might support negative stereotypes and minimize particular demographic groups.

Guidelines for Fairness:

- **Diverse Training Data**: The training data for Qwen 2.5-Max must include wide-ranging information that correctly displays different population demographics together with standalone points of view and life experiences. The diversity implementation decreases the possibility of modified data influencing useless outcomes.
- **Bias Audits**: Regular bias audits should be conducted to check for any potential biases in the output of Qwen 2.5-Max. The system includes features to identify gender assumptions together with racial and cultural prejudices within language models.
- **Bias Mitigation**: Qwen 2.5-Max implements bias reduction techniques which include adversarial debiasing along with fairness constraints and bias correction algorithms that minimize output biases.

b. Fairness in Deployment

The recommendations system must deliver equal treatment to all users as well as user groups through non-discriminative outcomes that ignore personal traits and background and identity details.

Best Practices:

- **Avoid Harmful Content**: The generation of Qwen 2.5-Max software must avoid producing offensive content which attacks specified groups comprising sensitive characteristics including race gender or religious beliefs or sexual orientation.
- **Inclusive Language**: The model design should require inclusive language while eliminating discriminatory ideas that associate with harmful stereotypes throughout the system.
- **Addressing Edge Cases**: Regular tests must be conducted on a range of edge cases to validate model fairness when dealing with all users and scenarios for people from underrepresented or marginalized groups.

2. Transparency & Explainability

a. Transparency in AI Models

Real-time transparency must be provided to Qwen 2.5-Max users about its operational methods and database utilization together with the mechanism of decision-making processes. When users are not able to see what their AI systems perform or how they reach conclusions their trust diminishes and questions regarding system accountability emerge.

Guidelines for Transparency:

- **Explainable Outputs**: Qwen 2.5-Max requires developers to create explainable output capabilities because it functions as a large language model especially throughout high-stakes deployments (for example healthcare and legal advice).

- **Documenting Model Limitations**: The documentation of Qwen 2.5-Max needs to specify both strengths and weaknesses of the system with special emphasis on the model's capability to create mistaken or biased outputs. The system enables users to decide intelligently regarding both timing and usage of the model.

- **Disclose Data Sources**: Users must reveal which datasets Qwen 2.5-Max utilizes for fine-tuning and sensitive application deployment and especially highlight data elements that might result in biases or privacy-related issues.

b. Model Interpretability

The developers of Qwen 2.5-Max should enhance the interpretability features to enable end-users better understand how model processing affects input data to produce output results.

Best Practices:

- **Model Behavior Documentation**: The model needs proper documentation about how it reaches decisions with clear instructions for users to understand results especially when using the system for critical purposes.

- **Post-hoc Explainability Tools**: Post-hoc Explainability Tools that include LIME (Local Interpretable Model-Agnostic Explanations) and SHAP (SHapley Additive exPlanations) should be implemented to enable users to comprehend what leads to particular predictions or output responses.

3. Privacy & Data Protection

a. Data Privacy

Qwen 2.5-Max operates on extensive databases while user personal information needs to remain the highest priority. Users should ensure both sensitive data gets adequate protection against unauthorized access and their private information does not get mishandled by this AI solution.

Guidelines for Privacy:

- **Data Anonymization**: Any user data or inputs going through fine-tuning or model evaluation must be transformed into anonymous or aggregate forms to stop users from being identified individually.

- **Sensitive Data Handling**: The application should handle sensitive personal data only when it serves essential use cases but users must safeguard it properly.

- **Data Retention Policies**: The organization should develop specific rules to define the lifetime span of data storage together with rules about data collection methodology. The necessary data retention period should be observed before conducting a secure deletion of information.

b. Secure Data Storage and Transmission

Data must be protected by using strong encryption protocols which keep information safe when it travels between systems as well as when data remains idle in storage facilities. Organizations need access controls that protect their data from unauthorized persons.

Best Practices:

- **End-to-End Encryption**: Qwen 2.5-Max should apply TLS/SSL for end-to-end encryption of data moving between its API and other endpoint connections.

- **Data Encryption at Rest**: Model weights and user inputs together with all sensitive data must be stored in encrypted storage services to guarantee data protection.

- **Access Control**: The model alongside data together with all associated infrastructure must have strict authentication and authorization procedures to determine user access permissions.

4. Accountability & Governance

a. Ensuring Accountability

Qwen 2.5-Max needs to have defined systems for holding personnel responsible throughout its development life cycle and operational deployment. The responsible parties must determine which person or organization handles the AI system while also monitoring ethical standards as well as assuming responsibility for model results.

Guidelines for Accountability:

- **Clear Ownership**: Define the roles and responsibilities of developers, users, and stakeholders in the AI lifecycle, including who is responsible for addressing issues such as bias, misuse, or privacy concerns.

- **Monitoring and Reporting**: Organizations should both supervise model operation and document performance outcomes particularly during high-risk domain implementation. Develop a straightforward method which allows people to report system problems and biases together with deployment errors.

- **Human Oversight**: Employee oversight of Qwen 2.5-Max remains necessary to ensure proper human supervision during critical decision-making processes affecting population or community outcomes. People serving as a second level of control should have access to neutralize hazardous model predictions.

b. Responsible Use & Misuse Prevention

Qwen 2.5-MAX demonstrates substantial potential to be misused as an AI model. Protection systems need to exist to stop Qwen 2.5-Max from serving dangerous tasks or any type of malicious function.

Best Practices:

- **Use Case Restrictions**: Qwen 2.5-Max requires specific limitations on how the system can be used to prevent unacceptable scenarios. The model should not be used as a tool to create misleading information because this would violate ethical guidelines.

- **Safeguards Against Harm**: The system must contain protective measures to detect dangerous or unsafe outputs and prevent their display to users including hate speech as well as disinformation and offensive material.

- **User Agreement and Ethics Training**: User agreements that cover ethical policies accompany authorization access to Qwen 2.5-Max through Application Programming Interfaces and other tools where all users must complete a responsible use ethics training.

5. Environmental Impact

a. Energy Efficiency

The training processes together with operational needs for large language models such as Qwen 2.5-Max demand substantial energy consumption that creates environmental concerns. AI technology must receive energy efficiency optimizations and assessments of its carbon emissions need consideration.

Best Practices:

- **Efficient Model Deployment**: The deployment of models should take advantage of efficient hardware together with cloud-based services that enable access to energy-efficient GPUs or TPUs in order to minimize energy usage during operation.

- **Model Optimization**: Model Optimization techniques including model pruning together with quantization and distillation help decrease computational requirements so energy usage decreases during model deployment and inference.

- **Sustainability Initiatives**: Training and deploying large AI systems should use sustainable renewable energy sources as a sustainability initiative to balance their environmental impact.

Conclusion

Qwen 2.5-Max along with other AI systems need responsible practices for their ethical operation as well as their fair and safe usage. Users and developers who emphasize fairness together with transparency alongside privacy and accountability and environmental impact minimization will decrease risks while maximizing helpful AI applications. Qwen 2.5-Max receives ethical guidelines that help developers deploy this AI system toward social values and ethical principles to benefit all stakeholders while minimizing harm.

CHAPTER TEN

RESOURCES & SUPPORT

Official Documentation Links for Qwen 2.5-Max

Official documentation for Qwen 2.5-Max offers essential details which require your reference for gaining accurate and up-to-date information. Official resources which document the Qwen 2.5-Max model can be accessed through the following pertinent links.

1. Official API Documentation

- **Link**: Qwen 2.5-Max API Documentation
  - o Provides detailed information on accessing Qwen 2.5-Max via API, including authentication, API endpoints, parameters, and usage examples.

2. SDK Documentation

- **Link**: Qwen 2.5-Max SDK Documentation
  - o Clients can discover documentation almost the SDK for consolidating Qwen 2.5-Max into their applications through different programming dialect cases such as Python and JavaScript.

3. Model Architecture and Parameters

- **Link**: Qwen 2.5-Max Architecture Documentation
  - ○ The documentation clarifies how Qwen 2.5-Max works by displaying its parameters along side preparing methodologies and optimization strategies.

4. Installation and Setup Guide

- **Link**: Qwen 2.5-Max Installation Guide
  - ○ Qwen 2.5-Max establishment direct presents a point by point strategy to setup the computer program locally and through cloud stages.

5. Responsible AI Guidelines

- **Link**: Qwen 2.5-Max Responsible AI Documentation
  - ○ Beneath the Dependable AI Guidelines section the documentation gives moral direction which prioritizes reasonableness at the side protection measures and straightforwardness in Qwen 2.5-Max utilize and abuse anticipation.

6. Troubleshooting and Common Issues

- **Link**: Qwen 2.5-Max Troubleshooting
  - A careful record giving arrangements for standard issues that show up amid Qwen 2.5-Max setup and establishment in expansion to its utilization handle.

7. User Guide for End-Users

- **Link**: Qwen 2.5-Max User Guide
  - This direct gives end-users with total data almost utilizing the show together with best hones and execution upgrade strategies and utilization strategy.

8. Community and Support

- **Link**: Qwen 2.5-Max Community Forum
  - Qwen 2.5-Max incorporates a community stage for users to trade questions and arrangements as well as tips with other demonstrate clients. Clients can report issues and ask highlights here in expansion to other client capacities.

9. Frequently Asked Questions (FAQ)

- **Link**: Qwen 2.5-Max FAQ
  - A report contains answers to visit questions around Qwen 2.5-Max managing with establishment direction and mistake resolutions and prevalent application strategies.

The intermittently overhauled assets give you with get to to the foremost later highlights as well as bug fixes and best hones for useful Qwen 2.5-Max operations.

Qwen 2.5-Max Community Forums

Through Qwen 2.5-Max Community Gatherings clients can communicate with each other whereas they inquire questions, give arrangements, trade bits of knowledge and create best hones for utilizing the show. The underneath list contains fundamental data with respect to the Qwen 2.5-Max community gatherings nearby their individual joins:

1. General Discussions

- **Link**: Qwen 2.5-Max General Discussion Forum
  - The common Qwen 2.5-Max client discourse forum features user stories in

conjunction with valuable tips and discourses with respect to usefulness and application zones of both the Qwen adaptation and capacity.

2. Troubleshooting & Bug Reports

- **Link**: Qwen 2.5-Max Troubleshooting Forum
  - o Clients in this gathering share found bugs, proposed fixes, and exchange information around standard establishment and utilization issues with Qwen 2.5-Max. The community individuals together with improvement staff work together to discover arrangements for detailed issues.

3. API & SDK Support

- **Link**: Qwen 2.5-Max API & SDK Forum
  - o Clients can get to Qwen 2.5-Max API & SDK assets through the Qwen 2.5-Max API & SDK Gathering. Engineers can utilize this gathering space to posture technical questions nearby the sharing of code pieces and settling of integration issues related to the Qwen 2.5-Max API and SDK.

4. Use Case Sharing

- **Link**: <u>Qwen 2.5-Max Use Cases Forum</u>
  - The gathering investigates diverse mechanical applications for utilizing Qwen 2.5-Max. Clients from distinctive foundations appear their project-specific cases beside their Qwen 2.5-Max application stories and how this arrangement benefits their work.

5. Model Fine-Tuning & Customization

- **Link**: <u>Qwen 2.5-Max Fine-Tuning Forum</u>
  - The gathering serves clients who wish to refine Qwen 2.5-Max particularly for specific assignments or segment applications. Through the gatherings individuals trade procedures and tips as well as portray their victory with altering the show to coordinate their details.

6. Best Practices & Responsible AI

- **Link**: <u>Qwen 2.5-Max Responsible AI Forum</u>
  - The Qwen 2.5-Max Responsible AI Forum hosts discussions about ethical AI practices for responsible deployment and fairness and

bias reduction in Qwen 2.5-Max software. Users gather in this platform to exchange perspectives that enhance ethical AI deployment.

7. Announcements & Updates

- **Link**: Qwen 2.5-Max Announcements Forum
  - The user needs to remain informed about current Qwen 2.5-Max releases and maintenance updates and platform news included in the forum. The development team releases essential updates about the platform together with new functionality and previews forthcoming product improvements on this forum.

8. Feature Requests & Feedback

- **Link**: Qwen 2.5-Max Feature Requests Forum
  - The discussion board allows Qwen 2.5-Max users to bring forward their proposals for new features and enhancements and development improvements. The team continuously tracks this forum for receiving valuable suggestions from users.

9. Community Events & Meetups

- **Link**: Qwen 2.5-Max Community Events
  - o Users can obtain information about Qwen 2.5-Max related community events as well as webinars and hackathons along with meetups through the official platform. The platform serves as an excellent way to participate with the community through both physical meetings and digital sessions.

Through these platforms users can work together as well as learn and exchange information with other members of the Qwen 2.5-Max user community. Such forums serve as essential resources for debugging help and updated information and skills development with the Qwen 2.5-Max model.

www.ingramcontent.com/pod-product-compliance
Lightning Source LLC
LaVergne TN
LVHW022124060326
832903LV00063B/3637